Cooking Secrets
From Acadiana's Award-Winning Chefs

American Culinary Federation, Acadiana Chapter

Anne Darrah, Cover and Divider Art
Amanda Griffin, Writer
DFP, Book Design

TRADERY
H·O·U·S·E

Library of Congress Card Catalog Number: 94-61904
ISBN 1-879958-25-2

First Printing   10,000   February 1995
Second Printing   10,000   April 1995

For additional copies, use the order form in the back of the book,
or call
The Wimmer Companies, Inc., 1-800-727-1034.

Printed in the USA by
WIMMER
The Wimmer Companies, Inc.
Memphis • Dallas

Contents

 indicates light suggestions

Preface

South Louisiana is one of the places in America that has a truly ethnic food heritage. It has been influenced by people from Africa, France, Spain, and the Caribbean. The American Culinary Federation, Acadiana Chapter, wanted to build on this heritage when it began the Culinary Classic in 1983. The Classic has enabled our local chefs, as well as those outside the area, to stretch their food heritage into the realm of haute cuisine without ever losing touch with their Louisiana roots.

This cookbook brings to the chef at home the best that the Culinary Classic winners have to offer. We've included actual award-winning recipes from the Classic (look for the pages highlighted with the medal) and recipes that these same chefs enjoy using at home. It's one thing to prepare an extraordinary dish of great complexity for a competition, but it's another to prepare something delicious day after day at home. Many of these chefs are sharing their favorite recipes, along with some of the "revelations" that make them wonderful. It's almost like standing at the chefs' elbows watching while they cook.

The ACF, Acadiana Chapter, is proud to share these recipes with you. Some of the techniques and recipes found in these pages are the same ones members of the 1996 ACF Culinary Olympic Team have come to Lafayette to learn from our chefs. We hope you enjoy a taste of Acadiana.

Acknowledgments

Many thanks are needed here. The cookbook would not be possible without all the chefs who contributed. Besides offering the recipes that have been award winners in the Culinary Classic over the years, the chefs each submitted 4 to 10 recipes they cook at home. Thanks also to the ACF members who served on the cookbook committee, especially those who spent extra hours meeting and gathering material.

A special note of appreciation goes to Linda Vincent-Broussard, Ed.D., Director of the School of Human Resources at the University of Southwestern Louisiana. She is not only my partner in life, but she has also been my partner in the development of the Culinary Classic to its present level of excellence. Because of her academic background and her experience at the management level at Walt Disney World, she brought a high degree of organization to the Culinary Classic. I am extremely grateful for her help.

Thanks also to those Acadiana residents who worked on other aspects of this project: Renee Durio, who helped plan the cookbook and coordinated the collection and organization of all material; Amanda Griffin, who diligently researched and wrote the editorial material for the front of the book; and Anne Darrah, who spent endless hours designing and refining the cover to satisfy her expectations and ours.

JOE BROUSSARD, PRESIDENT
American Culinary Federation, Acadiana Chapter

Introduction

By Amanda Griffin

Roots of the Culinary Classic

IN 1980, Louisiana Chef Paul Prudhomme ignited America's taste buds and his black iron skillet with Blackened Red Fish, and a new eating craze was born. What people across America didn't know, but television chef and joke teller Justin Wilson had been saying for years, was that folks in South Louisiana have always known how to cook—and eat.

So in 1983 in Lafayette, Louisiana, only 20 miles from Prudhomme's hometown of Opelousas, the Acadiana Culinary Classic was created. It was designed by the Acadiana Chapter of the American Culinary Federation (ACF) as an annual showcase for the professional chefs who truly knew the secrets of real Louisiana food. The timing for the first Culinary Classic was perfect because Louisiana food was popping up on menus from coast to coast, even if it was nothing more than a steak doused in hot sauce. The folks of Lafayette embraced the first Culinary Classic as a fund raiser for the Louisiana Chapter of the National Hemophilia Foundation and as a chance to enjoy the best recipes created by their favorite local chefs. Some 32 chefs participated, presenting such regional specialties as Crawfish Étouffée, Oyster Andouille Gumbo, and Cajun Roast Duck with Oyster Dressing. From that first year the Culinary Classic had the makings of a truly successful food competition. First, the people of Acadiana are passionate about their food and eat with gusto. There is no occasion in South Louisiana—social, business, or otherwise—that doesn't hold the possibility for some type of food to be prepared and enjoyed. Secondly, the food in Acadiana is some of the best in the world. It may be as simple as a perfectly fried piece of catfish, or as complex as a bowl of steaming seafood gumbo that leaves you wiping up the last drop with a crust of French bread and wondering, "What made that so soul-satisfying and delicious?" The Culinary Classic gave regional chefs the opportunity to put their memorable food in the spotlight.

Each year the Culinary Classic grew. By the second year the number of competing chefs had jumped to 55, and the Best of Show medal went to Chef Patrick Mould for his Redfish Louisiane, which featured a fried filet of fish with a crawfish sauce similar to an étouffée. The dish was something of a culinary road sign that pointed to a new direction for traditional Cajun cooking in Lafayette. Sautéing and using sauces was being done routinely across the country, but in Lafayette much of the food was still fried or prepared in traditional dishes like gumbo. Mould's dish was a sign that local chefs were willing to take their Cajun culinary roots and meld them with new techniques and foods. The result was something familiar, yet with a new twist. Ten years later this direction has a name, "fusion food," represented by the recipes prepared at the Culinary Classic. The food has become more complex without forsaking its Cajun roots.

The ACF, Acadiana, added a cooking seminar to the Culinary Classic in 1989. The public bought tickets and came in large numbers to watch and learn from chefs Paul Prudhomme, Bernhard Gotz of Mother's Restaurant; and Joe Cahn, owner of the New Orleans School of Cooking; and to hear the music of New Orleans pianist Ronnie Kole, who has been at every Classic. The seminar was deemed a success and became an annual event that features nationally known chefs.

In 1990 the Culinary Classic gained a new beneficiary, the Junior League of Lafayette. Ticket sales jumped to more than 900, and the Classic was held at the Lafayette Cajundome. Conceived and organized by Linda Vincent-Broussard, Le Petite Classique, a competition for children, appeared in 1992. The Classique encourages young chefs to consider a future in the cooking or hospitality industry.

The Culinary Classic has become a Lafayette tradition, and a means of churning charity dollars back into the community through the ACF. But it has also become a point of pride for the regional chefs who compete . Through the years they have refined their skills, learned new methods of presentation, and earned money and recognition for their efforts. Beginning several years ago, chefs can now compete for points and medals in official ACF divisions of the Culinary Classic, which are judged by certified ACF judges. With the strides the Culinary Classic has made in its first 10 years, Joe Broussard, chairman, hopes that in the next 5 years the prize money for Best of Show will be $25,000.

Unlocking the Cajun Secrets

As a newlywed moving to Lafayette from Alabama, I figured Louisiana couldn't be too different from my home state because geographically it is also part of the Deep South. But, what I didn't know about the culture of Acadiana were things a map could never tell me. My introduction to the French culture of the area came swiftly and in unexpected ways. Our neighbors' last name was Fuselier, but that was only the first of many new surnames I had to learn. I had to write the French names phonetically while I searched for a job so that my Alabama-born tongue wouldn't bungle a potential employer's name. I occasionally shopped for groceries at a small family-owned store on North Moss Street. The old timers spoke French to one another as they shopped, and the shelves were filled with their favorite ingredients. I marveled at the huge 10-pound bags of rice, especially short grain, the preferred variety of the Cajuns because it sticks together so well and is the perfect bed for a blanket of brown gravy. There were jars of Savoie's Roux, a dark chocolate-colored mixture with a layer of oil floating on top. I had no idea what to do with it.

When it comes to learning something new, a mentor always helps. In my case, it was my husband's cousin, Effie Mouton of Lafayette. Even today, Effie, in her eighties, cooks and entertains. It was due to Effie and her husband, Charlie, that I learned some of the secrets of this new culture. A visit to their house was never complete without a demitasse of dark roast Community coffee or a glass of wine or beer. You couldn't sit in their living room for even 10 minutes without Charlie ambling toward the kitchen to serve refreshments. It was from Effie that I learned to smother chicken, a dish so simple that you wonder why the whole world doesn't know about it. The browning chicken and the sautéing green peppers and onions send up an aroma that makes you hungry. She even shared a secret with me as I grappled with the task of making my first roux for a gumbo. Kitchen Bouquet, a pantry staple from a generation ago, is the perfect way to darken a roux that doesn't quite reach that highly prized, deep-chocolate brown color. But I learned more than that from Effie and Charlie. Over the years watching them open their home to kith and kin for Mardi Gras, birthdays, or any other occasion, I learned something about the French Louisiana spirit of sharing. No one comes in their door without receiving refreshment; what is theirs is yours.

Food Is a Way of Life in Acadiana

In 1755 the French living in Acadie, Nova Scotia, were expelled from their land by the British. By boat or by foot, many of them arrived in South Louisiana to be welcomed by the French already here. The Spanish, then in control of the territory, provided land grants to the Acadians. The story is told that when the French, or Cajuns as they became known, left Nova Scotia they took with them a lobster from the cold, Northern waters. As they made their way to their new home, the lobster gradually grew smaller and smaller until it was only a crawfish. The crawfish, like the Cajuns, survived the long, often treacherous journey. The crawfish story is only folklore, but what is fact is that the Acadians survived their rude upheaval to populate a rich and wild territory that remained largely untouched by the modern world until roads reached deeper into the area in the 1930s. What is also true is that approximately 90% of the United States' supply of crawfish comes from Cajun country. No where else in the world has the crawfish become such a prominent part of a regional cuisine.

But the crawfish is just one example of the way the Cajuns learned to use the foods available to them. The rivers and swamps provided an abundance of fish, shellfish, and game, while the prairies of southwestern Louisiana eventually yielded rice and other crops. The families developed a deep kinship as they came to depend upon one another for a variety of needs. For example in cold weather, Cajuns from several farms would get together for a *boucherie*, the butchering of a hog. The families would work and visit, and at the end of the day there would be time to eat the cracklins, smothered debris, boudin, smoked sausage, and backbone stew made during the day. A bit of fiddle music, a little dancing, good food, and fellowship made for a rich day, and to top it off, everyone went home with some of the byproducts of the butchering.

So What Is Cajun Food?

The French living in New Orleans had brought their chefs with them, while the Spanish brought theirs years later. The Acadians settled along the bayous and swamps and cooked with what was at hand. Also in the area were slaves, many who had come directly from such exotic homelands as Senegambia, the Windward Coast of West Africa, Martinique, and Haiti. Mix all of those influences and you reap what has become known as Cajun cuisine, actually a unique blend of many forces. And like a good roux, the blending is so thorough it's impossible to see where one ingredient ends and another begins. Cajun cuisine, then and now, has been one of improvisation and necessity. While the French, or Creole, cuisine of New Orleans maintained its close alliance with France, and consisted of fine sauces and sophisticated tastes, the Cajun matron of the bayous and prairies had to be more practical. The Cajun style became the difference between city cooking and country cooking, some authorities have said. It's the difference between using many pots, and the economy of cooking everything in one pot, as for a Cajun jambalaya. But because Cajun is a word that has been bastardized, it's no wonder that people often approach the real cuisine with some trepidation. Visitors to South Louisiana often expect everything from the scrambled eggs to dessert to be laced with so much red pepper that a fire extinguisher must be kept near at hand. It's a shame that Cajun has come to mean "hot." Sure, the food is usually well spiced with everything from red pepper, to salt, to hot sauce, to bay leaves and ground sassafras leaves. But, additional flavor is gained from the "Holy Trinity" of ingredients—the onion, bell pepper, and celery—that is used in almost every Cajun dish. Garlic, parsley and chopped green onion tops add depth of flavor. More recently basil, thyme, oregano, onion powder, and cardamom are accepted as ingredients in nouveau Cajun cuisine. And, by the way, blackening is not a Louisiana technique; Chef Paul Prudhomme will tell you that himself. It is based, however, on that most important of ingredients—ingenuity. Suffice it to say, Cajun cuisine was not a fad. It is now a recognized regional cuisine unique to South Louisiana. Fine restaurants across the country draw upon the seasonings and cooking techniques of Cajun foods to enhance their menus.

First You Make a Roux

The most common expression you'll hear in Cajun country is, "first you make a roux," which is a cooked mixture of flour and oil, although in generations past, animal fat was used. Making a roux is one of those culinary arts that varies from kitchen to kitchen. Most cooks learned to make one by stirring the mixture over a low flame in a black iron skillet for at least an hour. It would gradually turn from light brown to caramel to deep brown. The lighter roux works best with dark meats, and the darker more robust one with lighter meats. Over the years commercial rouxs have been bottled, which even the most die-hard of Cajun cooks have embraced happily. Other cooks have shortened the process by heating the oil to a high temperature, adding the flour, and then stirring like crazy for 5 minutes or less until the right color is achieved. This takes the savvy of a magician because the roux can easily burn and lend a bitter taste to the final dish. With the need to lighten up on the fat in many Cajun recipes, some chefs devised roux made only from browned flour.

A roux is often followed by the addition of chopped onion, bell pepper, and celery, usually with minced garlic added. That is the basis for many a fine Cajun dish. From there, the ingredients can be as varied as what's in the barnyard, bayou, or freezer. Cajuns have the reputation of eating most anything that doesn't first eat them. There's not a wild animal that hasn't found its way into a gumbo pot at some time or another, and when meat is scarce, a gumbo can be made with a variety of greens for Gumbo Z'Herbes.

When a Cajun gets ready to cook, it usually means getting out his biggest pot. Cajuns like their black iron Dutch ovens and skillets, but Magnalite is a close second. You might note that these are very heavy cooking utensils; anything too thin will never hold up when it comes to making a roux. Cajuns are inventive. They will make barbecue grills out of huge galvanized metal drums, or a "Cajun microwave" out of a metal-lined, wooden box. The name of the game is creation and ingenuity. And their motto might be, "If he can cook it, I can cook it better." With the revelations shared in this book by the award-winning Culinary Classic chefs, you too can cook it better—and cook it Cajun.

ACADIANA REGION OF LOUISIANA

Culinarians' Code

I pledge my professional knowledge and skill to the advancement of our profession and to pass it on to those who are to follow.

I shall foster a spirit of courteous consideration and fraternal cooperation with our profession.

I shall place honor and the standing of our profession before personal advantages. I shall not use unfair means to effect my professional advancement or to injure the chances of another colleague to secure and hold employment.

I shall never expect anyone to subject to risks which I would not be willing to assume myself.

I shall help to protect all members against one another from within our profession.

I shall be just and enthusiastic about the success of others as I m about my own.

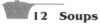

GOLD—1993

BEST OF SHOW

Roasted Three-Pepper Soup with Crabmeat and Fennel

3 red bell peppers
3 yellow bell peppers
3 green bell peppers
2 pounds butter
2 bulbs of shallots, finely diced
1 bulb fennel, julienned
1 clove garlic, chopped
1 cup flour
1 quart chicken stock
1 quart heavy cream
Salt to taste
White pepper to taste
1 cup dry vermouth
1 pound lump crabmeat
1 tablespoon crème fraîche or a dab of sour cream

Roast peppers on a baking sheet in the oven at 350° until skins char. Cool, peel, and remove seeds; chop each color pepper separately, and set aside. In a stockpot, sauté shallots and fennel with garlic until clear. Add flour, and cook for 2 minutes. Add chicken stock and heavy cream. Lightly season with salt and white pepper. Divide mixture into three pots, and add a group of peppers to each. Puree each mixture until smooth. Return each pot to the stove. (Soups must all have same consistency, so if one is thinner, combine a small amount of flour and melted butter, and very slowly add to soup. If needed, add salt and pepper to each.) Cook each pot for 10 minutes. Then add ⅓ cup of vermouth to each pot; cook for 2 minutes, or until wine evaporates. Divide crabmeat into individual shallow bowls. Taking ½ cup of each of the pepper soups, pour all three over crabmeat at same time. (If they are the same consistency, they will stay separate.) Garnish each serving with crème fraîche.

Yield: 10 servings
Derrick Trotter

Garnish each serving with fennel leaf, if desired. Crème fraîche can be purchased in gourmet markets.

secretsecretsecretsecretsecretsecretsecretsecretsecretsecretsecretsecretsecret

The roasted pepper flavor added to the delicacy of the crabmeat gives the dish a down-to-earth feeling even though the presentation is fancy.

Bacon and Leek Potato Bisque

8 slices bacon
2 leeks, sliced (use
  mostly white)
1 pound butter
1 cup flour
1 quart water
1 tablespoon chicken
  base (Minor's) or
  bouillon cubes (2-3)

4 small potatoes,
  peeled and diced
1 pint heavy cream
Salt to taste
White pepper to taste
Dash of nutmeg

Sauté bacon and leeks in a stockpot. Pour off half the bacon grease, and add butter until butter melts. Add flour, and cook for 2 minutes. Stir in water, chicken base, potatoes, and cream. Add salt, white pepper, and nutmeg to taste. Bake at 325° until potatoes are tender. Remove from oven, and cool slightly. Puree mixture until smooth.

Yield: 6 servings
Derrick Trotter

This soup can be served either hot or cold. Cut leaves of leek into small diamond-shaped pieces; blanch until tender and use to garnish soup.

Shrimp and Artichoke Bisque

½ pound butter
1 onion, chopped
1 red bell pepper,
  chopped
1 rib celery, chopped
1 cup flour
1 quart water

3 small cans artichoke
  hearts, drained and
  chopped
1 pound small bay
  shrimp
2 teaspoons McCormick's
  Season-All
1 pint heavy cream

Substitute margarine for butter, reduce flour to ½ cup, and use 1 cup half-and-half instead of heavy cream.

Melt butter in a stockpot over medium heat. Add onion, bell pepper, and celery; sauté for a few minutes. Stir in flour. Add 1 quart water, whisking ingredients together. Add artichokes, shrimp, and seasoning. Heat until thickened. Add heavy cream, and heat until shrimp are cooked. If not thick enough, stir a little cornstarch and water together and add to the bisque, mixing thoroughly.

Yield: 10 servings
Bill Bell

This is a simple dish that tastes great as is or served over pasta.

This was first made from leftover shrimp étouffée, and 6 gallons sold in 30 minutes.

Oyster and Tasso Soup

Omit cream, and use Milnot evaporated milk. Use turkey tasso. Omit butter and flour, and thicken with cornstarch and water.

1 stick of butter or margarine
2 large onions, diced
1 pound tasso, diced
1 green pepper, diced

2 tablespoons garlic, minced
1 cup flour
4 pints oysters
1 ½ quarts heavy cream
Salt and pepper

Melt butter in a stockpot. Add next 4 ingredients, and sauté. Add flour, and make a light-colored roux. Drain oysters, and add juice to the roux. Add heavy cream and salt and pepper to taste. Simmer 45 minutes. Add oysters, and turn off heat.

Yield: 10 servings
Bill Bell

Oysters should be added right before serving. Serve with garlic croutons on the side.

secretsecretsecretsecretsecretsecretsecretsecretsecretsecretsecretsecret
Use Richard's Cajun Country tasso for an authentic Cajun soup.

Reuben Soup

This delicious soup evolved from the chef's love of the sandwich of the same name. One day he had an urge to make the sandwich but had no rye bread. So he used all of the other ingredients and made them into a soup.

½ cup beef stock
½ cup chicken stock
¼ cup chopped onion
¼ cup chopped bell pepper
¼ cup chopped celery
1 tablespoon cornstarch
2 tablespoons water

1 cup shredded corned beef
1 cup shredded Swiss cheese
¾ cup sauerkraut, drained and rinsed
¼ cup butter
2 cups half-and-half
Salt to taste
Pepper to taste

Bring both stocks, onion, bell pepper, and celery to a boil in a Dutch oven. Simmer for 5 minutes. Mix cornstarch and water. Blend into stock. Simmer for 3 minutes (soup should thicken). Add corned beef, cheese, and sauerkraut. Melt butter in small saucepan, and add half-and-half; do not boil. Add to soup; stir until well blended. Season to taste.

Yield: 8 servings
Joseph Gonsoulin

Top individual bowls with rye bread and melted Swiss cheese.

Turtle and Okra Soup

SILVER—1992

3 tablespoons cooking oil
1 ½ pounds turtle meat, diced and seasoned
6 ounces tenderloin, diced and seasoned
2 teaspoons minced garlic
½ cup diced celery
½ cup diced bell pepper
1 cup diced onion
1 can tomato paste
1 can whole tomatoes
1 can Rotel tomatoes
1 quart beef stock
1 ½ cups okra, sliced
4 tablespoons dark roux
6 whole cloves
1 teaspoon sweet basil
1 teaspoon salt
1 teaspoon pepper
¼ cup chopped green onion
¼ cup minced parsley
½ cup sherry
10 slices boiled egg for garnish

Place oil in a deep stockpot. Once oil is hot, place meats in pot and brown. Add garlic, celery, bell pepper, and onion; then sauté. Add tomato paste and brown. Stir in the rest of the tomato products. Add stock and okra. Once it is boiling, stir in dark roux, cloves, basil, salt, and pepper. Add green onion and parsley. Let simmer for an hour. Add sherry. Garnish with egg, and serve.

Yield: 10 servings
Patrick Breaux

secretsecretsecretsecretsecretsecretsecretsecretsecretsecretsecretsecretsecret

Heat a little sugar in the oil before adding meats to help create caramel color.

Roasted Fennel and Crab Bisque

SILVER—1991

2 roots of fennel
2 ounces bacon, diced
1 ounce ham, diced
1 onion, chopped
1 bell pepper, chopped
1 garlic clove, chopped
4 ounces white wine
2 quart chicken stock
1 ounce butter
1 ounce flour
1 ounce mixed seasoning
½ quart heavy cream
1 pound lump crabmeat

Roast fennel until tender; chop. Cook bacon and ham in stockpot. Add vegetables and roasted fennel root. Cook until vegetables are clear. Add white wine and simmer. Add stock. Thicken with white roux made with butter and flour. Season. Add cream and crabmeat. Simmer for 20 minutes. Serve.

Yield: 10 servings
Patrick Breaux

Cream of Broccoli Soup

1 head of broccoli
1 quart water
1 medium onion, chopped
1/2 bell pepper, chopped
4 stalks of celery, chopped

1 pint milk
1 tablespoon chicken base or 2 chicken bouillon cubes
2 tablespoons Zatarain's Creole Seasoning
1/2 cup blond roux

Chop broccoli, and put in stockpot with water; boil for 20 minutes. Add onion, bell pepper, and celery; cook for 20 minutes or until tender. Add milk, chicken base, and seasoning; then thicken with roux.

Yield: 6 servings
Michael Chaisson C.W.C.

secretsecretsecretsecretsecretsecretsecretsecretsecretsecretsecretsecret

Zatarain's Creole Seasoning gives Cream of Broccoli Soup its special flavor.

Onion and Potato Soup

1 bell pepper
3 ribs celery
5 cloves garlic
3 ounces butter
1 ounce olive oil
4 large onions, finely sliced
3 large potatoes, unpeeled and finely sliced
Thyme to taste

2 bay leaves
Salt to taste
Black pepper to taste
6 ounces dry vermouth
1 1/2 quart chicken broth
1 cup beef broth
6 large slices of bread, toasted
6 ounces Swiss cheese, grated

Chop the bell pepper, celery, and garlic; sauté in butter and olive oil in stockpot until tender. Add finely sliced onions and potato, and sauté until onions are golden brown. Add thyme, bay leaf, salt, and pepper. Deglaze with dry vermouth; add chicken broth and beef broth. Cook for 35 minutes. Pour soup in individual bowls; place the toasted bread on top, and cover with Swiss cheese. Brown in the oven for 3 to 4 minutes.

Yield: 6 servings
Gilbert Decourt
This tasty soup goes well with a dry white Bordeaux.

Crème de Trois Legumes

2 ounces shallots	½ gallon chicken stock
1 ounce butter	Thyme and bay leaf to
1 ounce olive oil	taste
½ pound wild	Basil to taste (fresh)
mushrooms	Salt to taste
2 pounds regular	Pepper to taste
mushrooms	8 ounces cream
¼ cup white wine	

Sauté shallots in heavy stockpan in butter and olive oil until tender. Clean and slice mushrooms; add to shallots, and cook for a few minutes. Deglaze with white wine. Add chicken stock and seasonings, and cook for 40 minutes. Cool soup slightly, and blend in food processor until smooth. Add cream and a few chunks of butter before serving.

Yield: 10 servings

Gilbert Decourt

Make Crème de Carrotes the same as above, but use carrots instead of mushrooms. Crème de Celery uses celery instead of mushrooms.

Three-Bean Chili Chowder

1 large onion, chopped	1 (15-ounce) can black
1 clove garlic, chopped	beans, drained
2 tablespoons	2 (14½-ounce) cans
vegetable oil	stewed tomatoes
1 green or yellow	1 cup chicken stock or
pepper, chopped	broth
1 (16-ounce) can kidney	1 cup picante sauce
beans, rinsed and	2 teaspoons ground
drained	cumin
1 (15-ounce) can pinto	2 teaspoons chili
beans, drained	powder
	½ teaspoon salt

Sauté onion and garlic in oil in large stockpot or Dutch oven until tender. Add remaining ingredients, and bring to a boil. Reduce heat, and simmer approximately 10 minutes.

Yield: 8 servings

Lynn Epstein L.D.N., R.D.

If desired, garnish chowder with shredded Cheddar or Monterey Jack cheese, chopped fresh cilantro, green onion slices, or sour cream.

Sauté onion and garlic in ¼ cup chicken stock instead of oil.

Lynn's mom is a native Texan. This is one of her favorite recipes she shared with her daughter.

Cuban Black Bean Soup

This is a true Cuban recipe Lynn acquired from a friend who used to run a Cuban restaurant. She's now a local radio personality but still has a passion for cooking.

8 cups low-sodium chicken stock
1 ham hock
2 cups water
1 medium-size green bell pepper, chopped
1 medium-size yellow bell pepper, chopped
1 medium-size red bell pepper, chopped
4 (15-ounce) cans black beans
3 ribs celery, chopped
2 large onions, chopped
¼ cup fresh parsley, chopped
2 tablespoons lemon juice
2 tablespoons vinegar
4 cloves garlic, minced
1 teaspoon marjoram
¼ teaspoon red pepper
¼ teaspoon black pepper
1 teaspoon poultry seasoning
1 teaspoon cumin
2 tablespoons chili powder

Combine all ingredients in a large stockpot or Dutch oven. Simmer on medium heat for 30 minutes. Remove 1½ cups of mixture, and process in blender until smooth. Add back to the batch of soup to enhance body and texture.

Yield: 12 servings

Lynn Epstein L.D.N., R.D.

If desired, garnish with corn or flour tortillas, chopped fresh tomatoes, green onions, and cilantro.

Turtle Soup

1 pound boneless turtle meat (preferably loggerhead)
1 jumbo onion, minced
3 stalks celery, minced
½ cup butter
3 ounces beef base
1½ ounces lobster base
3 bay leaves
½ tablespoon oregano leaves
½ tablespoon thyme leaves
¾ ounce Tabasco
2 ounces Worcestershire
1 (10-ounce) can tomato sauce
2 quarts water
1 cup flour
2 cups water
¼ lemon (pureed in blender with a little water)
4 boiled eggs, peeled and chopped
¼ bag fresh spinach, chopped
½ cup cooking sherry

Brown first three ingredients in butter in large stockpot. Add next 8 ingredients and cook approximately 10 minutes. Stir often. Add 2 quarts water, and cook at medium high heat for 1 hour. Combine flour and 2 cups water, and slowly add to soup, whisking constantly. Cook for 20 minutes at medium heat. Remove from heat, and add last four ingredients before serving.

Yield: 8 servings
Eric Fincke

Shrimp and Okra Bisque

3 bay leaves
2 teaspoons salt
1 1/2 teaspoons dry mustard
1 1/2 teaspoons white pepper
1 teaspoon red pepper
1 teaspoon thyme
1/2 teaspoon black pepper
1/2 teaspoon basil
6 tablespoons vegetable oil, divided
3 cups okra, sliced and divided

3/4 cup chopped onion
3/4 cup chopped green bell pepper
1/2 cup chopped celery
1/4 cup butter
2 teaspoons chopped garlic
1/4 cup all-purpose flour
5 1/2 cups seafood stock
1/2 cup chopped green onions
1 pound shrimp (peeled)

Combine first 8 ingredients in a bowl for seasoning; set aside. Heat 4 tablespoons of oil in heavy 4-quart saucepan over high heat for 1 minute. Stir in 2 cups of okra, and sauté until brown. Add onion, bell pepper, and celery, and cook for 5 minutes. Add butter, garlic, and seasoning mixture, and cook for 5 minutes. Stir in flour and remaining oil. Continue cooking, stirring frequently until flour turns brown. Add stock and remaining okra and bring to a boil. Simmer for 10 minutes. Add green onions and shrimp, and cook for 3 minutes.

Yield: 8 servings
Joseph Gonsoulin

Serve over freshly cooked rice with French bread and a green salad.

secretsecretsecretsecretsecretsecretsecretsecretsecretsecretsecretsecretsecret

The roux, okra, and shrimp make this dish special. Remember when sautéing okra, be sure it is fresh and cooks long enough to avoid a slimy broth.

Cream of Chanterelles, Morels, and Andouille

¹/₄ cup margarine
²/₃ cup Vidalia onions
1 cup diced oak-smoked andouille sausage
4 cups fresh chanterelle mushrooms, sliced
4 cups fresh black morel mushrooms, sliced
¹/₄ cup Madeira wine
¹/₄ cup cream sherry
2 cups rich veal stock
3 cups heavy whipping cream
2 teaspoons sweet Hungarian paprika
¹/₈ teaspoon fresh ground black pepper
Pinch of cayenne pepper
Pinch of paprika
Pinch of salt
3 tablespoons cornstarch
¹/₄ cup water
Duck cracklin' or regular croutons

Melt margarine in heavy saucepan; sauté onion until translucent. Add sausage; sauté for 4 to 6 minutes until edges brown. Add mushrooms, and continue to sauté for 4 minutes. Deglaze pan with wine and sherry; cook until liquid is reduced by half. Add veal stock; reduce by a fourth. Add heavy cream; reduce by a fourth. Stir in Hungarian paprika, black pepper, cayenne pepper, paprika, and salt. Mix cornstarch and water, and use to thicken soup. Garnish each cup of soup with 3 to 4 croutons.

Yield: 10 servings
· James Graham

The first time James made this soup, he had some leftover fresh morel mushrooms, second in flavor only to truffles. This soup has since accompanied elk chops, rabbit, stuffed quail and venison, as a Gold Medal sauce as well as a delicate soup.

Chicken and Sausage Gumbo

James won first place in 1991, 1992, and 1993 in the World Champion Gumbo Cook-Off for this recipe.

3¼ cups oil, divided
3 cups flour
4 pounds boneless chicken, cut into 1-inch pieces
2 pounds smoked sausage, diced
3 cups diced onions
2 cups diced bell pepper
1 cup diced celery

1 gallon rich chicken stock
1 teaspoon liquid smoke
1 teaspoon Tabasco
1 tablespoon black pepper
2 teaspoons red pepper
1 tablespoon garlic powder
Green onion tops, chopped

First, make a roux: Heat 3 cups oil on medium in a large heavy pot. Add flour slowly, stirring constantly until dark brown in color; set aside but keep warm. In another large bottomed pot, heat ¼ cup oil over medium; add chicken, and brown for 10 minutes. Add sausage, and brown for 10 more minutes. Stir in onion, bell pepper, and celery until well blended, and cook for 10 minutes until vegetables are transparent. Add chicken stock, liquid smoke, and Tabasco; stir slowly until thoroughly mixed. Stir in black pepper, red pepper, garlic powder, and reserved roux; simmer on low for 45 minutes. Garnish with green onion tops. Serve over steamed rice.

Yield: 12 servings
James Graham

secretsecretsecretsecretsecretsecretsecretsecretsecretsecretsecretsecretsecret

This recipe has a little more roux than most gumbos and chicken base instead of salt.

Fennel and Saffron in a Velouté of Scallops

½ cup margarine	1¼ pounds scallops
2 pounds fennel, chopped	2 cups white wine
1 cup chopped onion	2 quarts water or seafood stock
1 cup chopped leek (white only)	Salt and pepper to taste
½ ounce saffron	Blond roux as needed
	2 cups whipping cream

Melt margarine in stockpot. Add fennel, onion, leek, and saffron; sauté until tender. Add scallops, and cook until slightly firm. Stir in white wine, and cook until reduced by a third. Add water, and bring to a boil; then return to a simmer. Season to taste. Remove from heat. Place in food processor; then strain. Return stock to the stove, and add roux to your desired consistency. Simmer 8 minutes. Add whipping cream, stir, and remove from heat. Set aside until ready to serve.

Yield: 10 servings
Michael Johnson C.W.C.

Leaves of Acadiana Pumpkin

2 tablespoons peanut oil	½ cup young pumpkin leaves
2 teaspoons finely diced shallots	1 tomato, peeled, seeded, and diced
1 teaspoon finely diced garlic	16 ounces coconut milk
2 medium shrimp (ground into a paste)	Salt to taste
	5 ounces shrimp (21-25 count), cleaned and deveined

Heat the oil in a shallow stockpot, and sauté the shallots and garlic for 2 minutes until glazed. Stir in the shrimp paste, and continue to sauté until thoroughly mixed. Blanch pumpkin leaves, and cut into strips. Add tomato and pumpkin leaves, and sauté for 8 minutes. Pour in the coconut milk, and bring to a boil. Reduce and simmer 10 minutes, stirring occasionally. Season with salt; then add shrimp. Continue to simmer 2 minutes. Remove the soup from pot, and pour into blender. Puree for 2 to 3 minutes.

Yield: 2 servings
Ken Koval

Alligator Cajun Cup

1 ½ pounds alligator meat, finely diced
4 ounces tasso meat, finely diced
1 quart alligator stock
1 quart veal stock
1 small sachet bag of herbs
1 medium shallot, finely diced
2 tablespoons butter
2 ounces dry vermouth
1 ounce dark roux
25 carrots, finely diced
25 celery, finely diced
25 leeks, finely diced
25 turnips, finely diced
Salt and pepper to taste

Brown alligator in 400° oven; then blanch in boiling salted water. Remove and put into stockpot with tasso, alligator and veal stocks, and sachet bag. Sauté shallot in butter for 1 minute; deglaze with vermouth, and reduce to half. Add to stockpot. Stir in roux. Blanch vegetables separately, and place in individual pieces of cheesecloth. Place all bags in stock, and simmer 30 minutes. Remove all bags from stock. Reduce stock to 1 ½ quarts. Strain and add to vegetables and meat. Season to taste with salt and pepper and serve.

Yield: 10 servings
Ken Koval

Crab and Corn Bisque

1 cup chopped onion
½ cup unsalted butter
2 (16-ounce) cans whole kernel corn, gently chopped in food processor
½ cup diced green bell peppers
1 quart heavy cream
3 teaspoons salt
½ teaspoon ground red pepper
½ teaspoon freshly ground black pepper
1 tablespoon parsley flakes
2 pounds lump crabmeat
2 tablespoons cornstarch
¼ cup water

Sauté onion in butter until tender. Add corn and bell pepper, and cook on medium-low heat for 20 minutes. Add heavy cream, salt, and next 3 ingredients; cook for 15 minutes. Stir in crabmeat, and cook for 5 minutes. Combine cornstarch and water, mixing well. Thicken bisque with cornstarch mixture.

Yield: 8 servings
William Menard

Potato Soup C. J.

½ cup margarine, melted
2 cups chopped onion
⅓ cup chopped celery
1 cup chopped green onion
1 teaspoon chopped garlic
½ cup chopped bell pepper
3 quarts water, divided
6 cups peeled, diced potatoes
4 cups peeled, cubed potatoes
2 pounds mixed sausage, thinly sliced
1 pound tasso, diced
4 cups peeled, wedged potatoes
4 tablespoons all-purpose flour
2 cups milk
1 (10¾-ounce) can cream of celery soup, undiluted
1 (10¾-ounce) can golden mushroom soup, undiluted
¼ cup chopped parsley
½ tablespoon dried basil leaves, crushed
2 teaspoons salt
2 teaspoons cayenne pepper

In a heavy stockpot, combine margarine, onion, celery, green onion, garlic, and bell pepper. Sauté 5 minutes until soft but not brown; Remove from pot, and set aside. Place 2 quarts water and 6 cups diced potatoes in pot; boil until tender on high heat. Mash potatoes down in water; add 4 cups cubed potatoes, 1 quart water, sausage, and tasso. Boil 20 minutes or until potatoes are tender. Add 4 cups wedged potatoes, and sautéed vegetables; mash well. In a small bowl combine flour and a small amount of the milk. Mix well, then add remaining milk (this keeps it from lumping). Add mixture to stockpot. Stir well, and cook on medium heat until potatoes are tender. Add cream of celery soup, cream of mushroom soup, parsley, and basil. Blend well, and add salt and cayenne pepper. Let simmer 10 minutes to let flavors blend together.

Yield: 12 servings
Chris Oncale

Corn and Crab Soup

1 stick butter
1 onion, diced
½ red bell pepper, diced
½ green bell pepper, diced
½ yellow bell pepper, diced
2 stalks celery, diced

1 teaspoon minced garlic
3 tablespoons flour
3 (11-ounce) cans whole corn, divided
2 cups half-and-half
2 cups heavy cream
1 pound crabmeat
¼ cup chopped green onions (optional)

In a large 3-quart stockpot, melt butter, and sauté diced onion and the next 5 ingredients, until onions are clear. Add flour, and mix well. Drain 3 cans corn, reserving liquid; set corn aside. Add liquid to stockpot, and whisk mixture with a wire whip. Add half-and-half then heavy cream, whisking constantly. When mixture is well combined, stir in half the corn. Reduce to a simmer. Meanwhile, in a food processor, puree the remaining corn. (This will be thick, so you can add ½ cup water or cream to thin it.) Using a strainer and rubber spatula, strain puree, and add smooth puree to soup. Add crabmeat, and stir gently. Simmer 10 minutes more and serve; garnish with green onions, if desired.

Yield: 8 servings
Lonnie Pope

This can be served as an appetizer with croutons.

secretsecretsecretsecretsecretsecretsecretsecretsecretsecretsecretsecret

Use crabmeat fresh from the waterways of Louisiana for the best flavor.

Enola's Turtle Soup

4 pounds boned-in
turtle meat
2 teaspoons lemon
pepper seasoning
2 teaspoons salt
1 teaspoon dried basil
leaves, crushed
1/2 teaspoon dried
thyme
1/2 teaspoon white
pepper
1/2 teaspoon red pepper
4 tablespoons butter
1/3 cup all-purpose flour
2 cups chopped red
onion
1 cup chopped celery

1/2 cup chopped bell
pepper
1/2 cup beef stock or
water
1 (6-ounce) can tomato
paste
1 1/2 cups tomato sauce
3 bay leaves
1 fresh clove garlic,
finely chopped
1 cup finely chopped
green onion
1/4 cup fresh parsley,
finely chopped
Juice of half a lime
1/3 cup dry sherry

In a large bowl, add the turtle meat. Sprinkle the next 6 ingredients over the meat, and mix well. Set aside to marinate for 1 hour. Melt the butter in a large Dutch oven over high heat. Add the marinated meat; cook and stir 15 minutes or until meat is browned on all sides. Remove the meat, and set aside. In the same pot gradually add the flour, stirring constantly for 5 to 8 minutes or until roux turns reddish-brown in color. Return the meat to the pot along with the red onion, celery, and bell pepper; continue cooking for 15 minutes, stirring to prevent sticking. Add the stock, tomato paste, tomato sauce, and bay leaves. Reduce the heat to medium, and cook for 1 hour or until meat is tender. Add the garlic, green onion, parsley, and lime juice. Cook an additional 10 minutes. Remove the meat from the pot, set aside, and let cool to touch; then debone meat (discarding bones). Cut meat into cubes, and return to pot. Add the sherry, and cook 1 minute longer. Remove from heat; discard bay leaves before serving.

Yield: 12 servings
Enola Prudhomme

Leek, Wild Mushroom, and Roasted Pepper Soup

1 red bell pepper
1 golden bell pepper
1 green bell pepper
2 quarts chicken stock, strained
1/2 cup diced red onions
1/2 cup diced yellow onions
2 cups leeks, halved and sliced
1/2 teaspoon white pepper

1/2 teaspoon cayenne pepper
1 tablespoon chopped garlic
2 cups wild mushrooms, cleaned and sliced
Cornstarch to thicken
2 tablespoons finely sliced chives

Roast peppers in oven on baking sheet until skins become charred. Tie peppers in brown paper bag until cool. Remove peppers; peel, remove seeds, and dice. Set peppers aside. In heavy stockpot combine chicken stock, red onions, yellow onions, and leeks. Bring to a simmer. Add white pepper, cayenne pepper, and garlic. Bring to boil; then lower heat to medium. Add wild mushrooms and peppers. Thicken with cornstarch. Garnish with chives. (Soup should be amber-colored, with all the different colors from the vegetables showing.)

Yield: 6 to 8 servings
Michael A. Richard

Serve in warm soup bowls with garlic croutons or fleurons.

secretsecretsecretsecretsecretsecretsecretsecretsecretsecretsecretsecret

Louisiana shiitake, chanterelle, and/or oyster mushrooms are best to use when they are available. Michael has a friend in Washington, Louisiana, who grows mushrooms, and he buys all he can to use at home and in the restaurant.

Gumbo Z'Herbes

6 chicken thighs
5 ounces Cajun smoked
  sausage, sliced
3 tablespoons oil
1 bunch green onions,
  finely minced
1 tablespoon sliced
  jalapeño pepper
1 tablespoon light
  brown roux
1 tablespoon gumbo
  filé powder
1 teaspoon freshly
  ground black pepper

1 dash crushed red
  pepper flakes
2 sprigs fresh thyme
  leaves
3 tablespoons of
  jalapeño juice from jar
Tabasco to taste
7 cups pure bottled
  uncarbonated water
½ pound whole spinach
  leaves, triple washed
  and destemmed
3 hard-cooked eggs,
  peeled and sliced

This recipe is true pioneer food. Believe it or not, the Cajun word Z'herbes means grass, hence the name for this greens gumbo.

Brown meats in oil; then add green onions and jalapeño pepper. Stir in roux, gumbo filé, black pepper, red pepper, and thyme. Add jalapeño juice and Tabasco. When mixture is nicely brown, add bottled water and spinach leaves. Simmer 30 minutes. Garnish with hard-cooked eggs.

Yield: 6 servings
Bryan Richard

Gumbo should be served over steamed rice or with corn-bread to dip. Leave Tabasco on the table.

secretsecretsecretsecretsecretsecretsecretsecretsecretsecretsecretsecretsecret

Tabasco is the key to this recipe.

Soupe des Fruits de Mer à la Tour d'Argent

This recipe is a salute to Tour d'Argent, the famous restaurant in Paris, France.

1 ½ white onions, chopped
1 red bell pepper, julienned
1 green bell pepper, julienned
1 yellow bell pepper, julienned
½ cup diced celery ribs
3 garlic cloves, chopped
1 cup sliced leeks
½ cup butter
Salt to taste
Cayenne pepper to taste
White pepper to taste
2 tablespoons whole saffron leaves

2 tablespoons roux
1 cup dry Sémillon wine
3 cups seafood stock
1 pound rainbow trout, scaled and cut into 2-inch pieces
1 pound swordfish, cut into 2-inch pieces
1 cup sea scallops, sliced
1 cup Gulf shrimp, deveined
1 cup heavy cream
3 tablespoons minced chives
18 puff pastry fleurons

In a large stockpot, sauté first 7 ingredients in butter until translucent. Stir in salt and next 4 ingredients. Add wine and stock, and bring to a boil. Add seafood, and simmer for approximately 8 minutes or until all seafood is cooked. Adjust consistency and texture and flavors as desired. Serve in individual soup bowls, and garnish with 3 puff pastry fleurons per serving.

Yield: 6 servings
Bryan Richard

Corn and Crab Bisque

2 tablespoons butter
½ cup finely chopped onion
½ cup finely chopped red bell pepper
¼ cup finely chopped green bell pepper
2 quarts heavy cream
2 quarts chicken stock
1 teaspoon seasoned salt
1 teaspoon white pepper
1 tablespoon garlic powder
1 tablespoon onion powder
1 teaspoon Tabasco
2 (16-ounce) cans whole kernel corn
2 (16-ounce) cans cream-style corn
¼ to ½ cup blond roux
1 pound crabmeat (backfin or white)
1 tablespoon thinly sliced green onions
1 tablespoon finely chopped parsley

Melt butter in an 8-quart saucepan or stockpot; add onion and peppers, and sauté until soft. Add heavy cream, chicken stock, seasoned salt, white pepper, garlic powder, onion powder, and Tabasco. Bring to a simmer. Add whole-kernel corn and cream-style corn. Stir to prevent scorching. Add blond roux until desired consistency is achieved. Add crabmeat, green onions, and parsley. Heat just until crabmeat is warmed throughout.

Yield: 10 servings
Michael A. Richard

Serve in warm bowls with crusty French bread. This cream soup is great with crawfish also.

You can use milk instead of heavy cream, but why change something that tastes so good.

The first time Michael made this soup for a family gathering, everyone thought it was the main meal and not just the first course. His Dad said he would be happy just eating the bisque, although he enjoyed everything else.

secretsecretsecretsecretsecretsecretsecretsecretsecretsecretsecretsecret

Tabasco and roux are the Cajun secrets.

Southwest meets Cajun in this expression of "fusion" cuisine.

Five Pepper Soup

2 tablespoons butter
1 onion, chopped
½ red bell pepper, julienned
½ green bell pepper, julienned
½ yellow bell pepper, julienned
2 jalapeño peppers, seeded and chopped
3 chile peppers, seeded and chopped
2 cups whole milk
10 ounces condensed chicken stock

1 (8¾-ounce) can whole kernel corn
1 cup shredded Monterey Jack cheese
2 dozen smoked oysters
1 tablespoon minced garlic
Red pepper
Black pepper
Oregano
Thyme
2 cups halved cherry tomatoes
10 sprigs parsley

Melt butter. Lightly sauté onion and peppers. Add milk, chicken stock, and corn. Cook 10 to 15 minutes at medium heat. Add Monterey Jack cheese. Melt. Add smoked oysters and garlic; add red pepper, black pepper, oregano, and thyme to taste. Cook 10 to 15 minutes more. When serving, add cherry tomatoes, and garnish with parsley.

Yield: 8 servings
Britt Shockley

Artichoke and Andouille Bisque

2 ounces unsalted
  butter
1/2 cup chopped bell
  pepper
1 cup chopped onion
2 ribs celery, chopped
1 gallon chicken stock
1/2 cup flour
1/2 cup oil
2 cups diced andouille
  sausage

2 cups artichoke
  quarters
1 tablespoon salt
1/2 tablespoon red
  pepper
1 tablespoon onion
  powder
1 tablespoon garlic
  powder
Parsley to garnish

Melt butter in stockpot, and sauté pepper, onion, and celery for 2 minutes. Add chicken stock, and bring to boil. Combine 1/2 cup flour and 1/2 cup oil to make a white roux. Add roux to stockpot. Whip mixture until thickened. Add andouille, artichokes, and seasonings, except parsley. Simmer 20 minutes, stirring frequently. Serve hot in large bowls, and garnish with parsley.

Yield: 10 servings
Chris Sogga

secretsecretsecretsecretsecretsecretsecretsecretsecretsecretsecretsecret
Andouille sausage and the Cajun "holy trinity" highlight this bisque.

Tomato and Crab Bisque

BRONZE—1988

8 cups water or seafood
  stock
1 cup blond roux
1 1/2 cups tomato paste
1/2 teaspoon cayenne
  pepper
1 tablespoon onion
  powder
1 tablespoon garlic
  powder
2 teaspoons salt

1 tablespoon chopped
  fresh basil
1 teaspoon fresh lemon
  thyme
1 tablespoon chopped
  green onions
1 tablespoon chopped
  fresh parsley
1/2 pound lump
  crabmeat

Bring water to a boil over medium heat. Mix in roux and tomato paste. Blend thoroughly. Add remaining ingredients, except crabmeat. Lower heat, and simmer for 10 minutes, stirring frequently. Add crabmeat about 3 minutes before serving.

Yield: 9 servings
Chris Sogga

Cream of Avocado and Lump Crabmeat

½ gallon shrimp stock
½ gallon crab stock
1 onion, chopped
1 bell pepper, chopped
1 rib celery, chopped
1 ounce crab base
1 cup blond roux
1 tablespoon onion
  powder
1 teaspoon garlic
  powder
1 teaspoon cayenne
  pepper
1 teaspoon black
  pepper
1 cup heavy cream
1 avocado, finely
  chopped
3 ounces lump
  crabmeat

Combine stocks, and bring to a boil. Add onion, bell pepper, celery, and crab base; bring to a boil. Stir in roux. Boil for 5 minutes on high; then lower heat and simmer. Add all seasonings and heavy cream. Simmer for 2 minutes. Fold in avocado and lump crabmeat; simmer to let flavors blend.

Yield: 10 servings
Chris Sogga

This is an excellent soup, but serve it with bread to combat the heat. Avocado can be pureed in food processor with a little stock for a smoother broth.

GOLD 1991

Salade Perigourdine

10 ounces pheasant
  breast
3 ounces mustard
10 ounces walnut oil
2 ounces vinegar
2 cups assorted greens,
  torn into bite-size
  pieces

10 ounces cèpes
  mushrooms, sliced
2 truffles, sliced
2 tomatoes, sliced
10 quail eggs, sliced
Salt and pepper to taste

Smoke the pheasant breast; then let it marinate for 30 minutes in a dressing made of mustard, walnut oil, and vinegar. Slice the pheasant. Combine pheasant, dressing, greens, mushrooms, tomatoes, eggs, and salt and pepper.

Yield: 10 servings
Gilbert Decourt

secretsecretsecretsecretsecretsecretsecretsecretsecretsecretsecretsecret

Truffles and cèpes make the difference in this recipe. Cèpes are the most powerful mushrooms on the market. Decourt gets these delicacies from his father who collects them in his hometown region of southwest France. Decourt is a longtime resident of Acadiana, so he combines French techniques with Cajun products for a wonderful marriage of flavors.

SILVER—1990

Smoked Seafood and Vegetable Salad

2 turnips
2 beets
2 carrots
1 zucchini
1 eggplant
1 head Belgium endive
1 head Boston lettuce
2 heads radicchio
4 (8-ounce) lobster
   tails
1 ounce crabmeat
2 ounces eel
1 ounce salmon
Mustard Herb Dressing
1 small can red caviar
   (garnish)
1 small can black caviar
   (garnish)
1 green onion, chopped

Peel, clean, and steam the turnips, beets, and carrots. Cut the zucchini into 1-inch pieces, and carve into oval shapes; then steam them. Grill the baby eggplant. Keep all the above vegetables in a cool place after cooking. Thoroughly clean the endive, Boston lettuce, and radicchio. Cold smoke the lobster tail with the crabmeat, eel, and salmon. Combine all the above ingredients on a platter, and top it with Mustard Herb Dressing. Garnish with caviars and green onions.

Mustard Herb Dressing:
1/2 cup olive oil
2 tablespoons Dijon
   mustard
2 tablespoons red wine
   vinegar
1 tablespoon chopped
   parsley
1 tablespoon chopped
   shallots
1 tablespoon chopped
   basil
Salt and pepper to taste

Combine all ingredients well. Serve over seafood and vegetable salad.

Yield: 10 servings
Gilbert Decourt

Fruit of the Sea

10 ounces scallops
10 ounces shrimp
(26 to 30 count)
10 ounces salmon
10 ounces crabmeat
10 ounces lobster
10 ounces mussels
5 1/3 cups olive oil
2 cups vinegar
6 tablespoons lime
juice
4 tablespoons Dijon
mustard
2 shallots, chopped
1 carrot, finely chopped
1 stalk celery, finely
chopped
1 leek, chopped
1 clove garlic, minced

2 tablespoons fresh
basil, chopped
2 tablespoons fresh
mint, chopped
1 tablespoon fresh
parsley, chopped
Salt to taste
White pepper to taste
2 heads radicchio, torn
into bite-size pieces
2 heads Bibb lettuce,
torn into bite-size
pieces
1 bunch watercress,
chopped
20 ounces puff pastry,
cut in squares and
baked according to
package directions

Poach all seafood; set aside. Combine olive oil and next 13 ingredients to make a mustard-vinaigrette dressing. Marinate seafood in dressing for 1 hour. Then serve with radicchio, Bibb, and watercress in puff pastry squares that have been cut horizontally to create a box.

Yield: 10 servings
Decourt Gilbert

Grilled Salmon and Mixed Greens

1 pound salmon fillets
2 red bell peppers
3 cups mixed greens
(red leaf, romaine,
and head lettuce)

1/2 cup sliced shallots
1/2 cucumber, sliced
1 cup commercial
honey-mustard
dressing

Grill salmon and peppers on an open grill until cooked. Peel peppers, and puree; set aside. Cut salmon into 1-inch pieces. Clean and cut all lettuce, and place on platter. Top lettuce with salmon, shallots, and cucumber. In a blender, slowly add roasted pepper puree to the honey-mustard dressing. Serve over salad.

Yield: 4 servings
Patrick Breaux

Venetian Salad

2 large eggplants
Roulades Stuffing
5 heads Belgian endive
2 heads radicchio
2 cups frisée
2 cups red leaf
5 cups mesclun
Dressing
10 ounces goat cheese
Croutons

Peel eggplants, and slice. Grill slices, and then place Roulades Stuffing in center of each; roll them up, and secure with a pick. Clean Belgian endive and next 4 greens; tear them into bite-size pieces, and place in a large bowl. Add eggplant roulades. Top salad with Dressing, and garnish with goat cheese and croutons.

Roulades Stuffing:

1 ounce olive oil
Juice of 3 lemons
1/3 cup diced shallots
1/4 cup diced mixed bell
    peppers
1 chile pepper, diced
1 tablespoon pine nuts
4 tablespoons
    Parmesan cheese
1 tablespoon chopped
    fresh basil
1 tablespoon chopped
    fresh mint
7 artichoke bottoms,
    chipped
2 whole tomatoes,
    chopped
10 ounces couscous
    grain
1 teaspoon minced
    fresh cilantro

Mix all ingredients well. Use to fill eggplant slices.

Dressing:

20 ounces olive oil
7 ounces balsamic
    vinegar
2 tablespoons minced
    fresh garlic
6 tablespoons minced
    fresh basil
9 sundried tomatoes
    (softened in boiling
    water for 5 minutes
    and then chopped)
1 teaspoon minced
    fresh cilantro

Mix all ingredients well. Pour over greens and eggplant roulades.

Yield: 10 servings
Gilbert Decourt

SILVER—1990

Shrimp and Artichoke Salad with Mustard and Pine Nut Vinaigrette

6 ounces shrimp (26 to 30 count)
1 cup artichoke hearts, chopped
$\frac{1}{2}$ (16-ounce) can of hearts of palm, sliced
$\frac{1}{2}$ head romaine lettuce, torn into bite-size pieces
6 leaves of radicchio, torn into bite-size pieces
1 carrot, peeled and sliced
2 hard-cooked eggs, peeled and sliced
10 cherry tomatoes, quartered
6 radishes, sliced
1 cucumber, sliced

Clean and cook shrimp; let cool. Combine shrimp with artichoke hearts and next 8 ingredients; mix well, and place on plate. Pour Mustard and Pine Nut Vinaigrette over salad, and serve immediately.

Mustard and Pine Nut Vinaigrette:

2 tablespoons red wine vinegar
1 teaspoon Dijon mustard
1 teaspoon chopped garlic
1 teaspoon salt
1 teaspoon black pepper
$\frac{1}{2}$ cup olive oil
1 teaspoon fresh basil
$\frac{1}{2}$ cup of pine nuts

In a small bowl, mix vinegar, mustard, garlic, salt, and pepper. Slowly pour in olive oil, and add basil and pine nuts. Pour dressing on salad.

Yield: 10 servings
Patrick Breaux

Spinach Salad with Lump Crabmeat

1 cup fresh spinach,
washed and torn
1 ounce cashews

2 ounces fresh lump
crabmeat

Combine all ingredients. Top with warm Bacon Vinaigrette. Serve immediately.

Bacon Vinaigrette:

1 cup bacon drippings
$^1/_3$ cup brown sugar

$^1/_3$ cup Grey Poupon
mustard
$^1/_2$ cup red wine vinegar

Heat bacon drippings to medium heat. Add brown sugar, stir till dissolved. Add mustard and whisk in red wine vinegar until all comes together.

Yield: 4 servings
Eric Fincke

Wilted Spinach and Lettuce Salad

5 ounces slab bacon
(cut into cubes)
3 tablespoons white
wine vinegar
1 $^1/_2$ teaspoons Dijon
mustard
9 tablespoons walnut
oil
Salt to taste
Freshly ground pepper
to taste

1 head red leaf lettuce,
cleaned and torn into
bite-size pieces
1 pound spinach leaves,
cleaned and torn into
bite-size pieces
$^1/_3$ cup walnuts,
chopped
1 shallot, minced

Fry bacon in skillet until golden but not crispy. Drain bacon on paper towels. Discard bacon fat. Stir vinegar into pan to deglaze it. Blend in mustard. Slowly whisk in walnut oil, until well emulsified. Season with salt and pepper. In a large bowl, toss red leaf lettuce with half of dressing. Arrange on serving platter. Heat remaining dressing in skillet; add spinach, and sauté quickly (about 1 minute). Place spinach over lettuce. Crumble bacon, and sprinkle over greens. Top with walnuts and shallots. Serve immediately.

Yield: 4 servings
Joe Gonsoulin

Tuna Seviche

Joe created this dish because he loves raw fish.

1 pound fresh tuna, cut into cubes	1 small red onion, chopped
2 tablespoons fresh lemon juice	1 large tomato, seeded and chopped
2 tablespoons fresh lime juice	3 tablespoons fresh cilantro, chopped
2 tablespoons vinegar	Salt to taste
2 teaspoons olive oil	Pepper to taste
2 teaspoons safflower oil	Tabasco to taste
	Cilantro sprigs
	Lemon and lime wedges

Combine first 12 ingredients together in a large bowl. Mix well. Cover tightly, and refrigerate for at least 8 hours. Divide mixture on 6 chilled plates. Garnish with a sprig of cilantro and lemon and lime wedges.

Yield: 6 servings
Joseph Gonsoulin

SILVER—1989

Fried Oyster Caesar Salad

12 oysters	1 head romaine lettuce, torn into bite-size pieces
2 eggs	
1 pint buttermilk	
Salt and pepper to taste	Dressing
	4 hard boiled eggs

Smoke oysters for 10 minutes. Mix batter of eggs and buttermilk; then season to taste. Dip oysters in batter, and fry for 2 minutes at 360°; set aside. Place romaine in large salad bowl. Toss romaine with dressing. Place oysters on salad, and garnish with egg wedges.

Dressing:

2 cups olive oil	2 teaspoon granulated garlic
1/2 cup lemon juice	
1/2 cup white wine vinegar	1 teaspoon salt
1 teaspoon black pepper	2 hard-cooked eggs, chopped

Mix all ingredients for dressing thoroughly before pouring over salad.

Yield: 10 servings
Wayne Jean

Mirliton Maurice

SILVER—1992

1 whole egg
2 slices beets
4 ounces juice from beets
2 ounces vinegar
1 clove garlic
Salt to taste
Pepper to taste
1 large mirliton (chayote)
Fresh chopped garlic to taste

Walnut oil to cover
Oregano to taste
Salt to taste
Pepper to taste
Coarse red pepper to taste
Mixed lettuces (frisée, red leaf, mesclun)
Radish sprouts
Cranberry Vinaigrette

This recipe is named for the farming community where the best mirliton were found for its creation.

Boil egg, and pickle with beets, juice of beets, vinegar, garlic, salt, and pepper for 24 hours before using. Poach mirliton in salted water until firm to the bite. Cool to room temperature. Marinate mirliton with finely chopped garlic, walnut oil, oregano, salt, pepper, and coarse red pepper for 24 hours before using. Drain mirliton well; cut into half, remove seed, and cut each half in half. Cut for fan presentation. Place on mixed lettuce, and garnish with wedge of pickled egg and radish sprouts. Top with Cranberry Vinaigrette.

Cranberry Vinaigrette:

12 ounces fresh cranberries
1 ounce sugar
½ tablespoon salt
½ tablespoon dry mustard

½ teaspoon sugar
White pepper to taste
½ cup vinegar cider
1½ cups peanut oil

Puree cranberries and 1 ounce sugar. Dissolve salt, dry mustard, ½ teaspoon sugar, and white pepper in vinegar. Combine with peanut oil, and mix vigorously.

Yield: 4 servings
Ken Koval

Grated garlic or grated onion (or both) may be added to the dressing.

Flower of the South

2 large tomatoes,
  blanched and peeled
4 medium-size red
  beets
1 head Bibb lettuce

1 head radicchio
  lettuce
16 enoki mushrooms
Eggplant Dressing

Cut tomatoes in half; hollow out. Boil red beets until tender; peel, let cool, and julienne. Wash lettuces, dry, and cut off bottom. Place lettuce leaves in each tomato half; add red beets and enoki mushrooms. Top with Eggplant Dressing.

Eggplant Dressing:

1 small eggplant
1 cup olive oil
Juice of 1 lemon
1 tablespoon dry
  mustard
2 shallots, chopped

2 sprigs parsley,
  chopped
$\frac{1}{2}$ tablespoon chopped
  garlic
Sparkling water
Salt to taste
Black pepper to taste

Pierce eggplant, and roast in 300° oven for 40 minutes. Cut in half, and remove as many seeds as possible. Scoop out meat of the eggplant, and puree with olive oil and next 5 ingredients for about 1 minute. Thin with sparkling water, as needed. Season with salt and pepper to taste.

Yield: 4 servings
Ken Koval

Shrimp, Corn, and Wagon Wheel Pasta Salad

4 teaspoons white wine
  vinegar
1 teaspoon chopped
  garlic
3 teaspoons fresh basil,
  chopped
3 teaspoons Dijon
  mustard
1 teaspoon hot sauce
$\frac{1}{4}$ teaspoon salt
1 teaspoon fresh thyme

1 teaspoon seasoning
  salt
1 cup olive oil
1$\frac{1}{2}$ pounds shrimp,
  cooked and cleaned
1 (16-ounce) can
  whole-kernel corn
8 ounces wagon wheel
  pasta, cooked
Lettuce leaves

In a food processor, blend vinegar and next 7 ingredients. Slowly add olive oil to the mixture. Mix the shrimp, corn, and pasta together in a large bowl. Add ingredients from the food processor, and blend well. Serve on a bed of lettuce, and garnish as desired.

Yield: 6 servings
Patrick Mould C.E.C.

Cajun Pâté with Bayou Dressing

GOLD—1988

2½ pounds ground pork
1 tablespoon Lea & Perrins
2 teaspoons Tabasco
1 tablespoon Tiger Sauce
1 tablespoon seasoning salt
1 teaspoon salt
2 tablespoons chopped garlic
½ cup chopped green onion
½ cup chopped parsley
18 strips bacon
2 strips of andouille sausage
2 (9-inch) strips of celery
4 strips red bell pepper
Lettuce leaves
Bayou Dressing

Lighten by using ground turkey instead of pork.

Combine first nine ingredients. Mix well. Line a 9x5x3-inch loaf pan with 14 strips of bacon. Do not overlap bacon but let it hang over sides. Divide pork mixture into 3 portions. Line bottom of pan with one portion spreading out to make an even layer. Place side by side 1 strip andouille, 1 strip celery, and 2 strips red bell pepper. Add another layer of pork mixture and another layer of andouille and vegetable strips. Top with last portion of pork mixture. Take bacon strips hanging over pan, and fold them over top of loaf; top with remaining 4 strips of bacon. Press firmly on mixture. Bake in water pan at 300° for 3 to 4 hours or until internal temperature is 180°. Weigh pan down by placing another loaf pan filled with weights on top. Chill in pan overnight. Serve slice of pâté on lettuce leaves and top with Bayou Dressing.

Bayou Dressing:

6 tablespoons capers, chopped
1 cup finely chopped celery
¾ cups parsley, finely chopped
½ cup finely chopped green onion
6 tablespoons lemon juice
1 tablespoon Tabasco
1 tablespoon Lea & Perrins
6 tablespoons ketchup
½ cup Dijon mustard
1½ tablespoons horseradish
3 cups mayonnaise

Combine first four ingredients; set aside. Combine lemon juice and remaining ingredients in mixing bowl. Add chopped ingredients, and mix well for 3 minutes or until blended.

Yield: 6 to 8 servings
Patrick Mould C.E.C.

secretsecretsecretsecretsecretsecretsecretsecretsecretsecretsecretsecret

This is a more traditional country French pâté, which is chunkier than most pâtés.

Cajun Smoked Beef Salad

This developed from leftover stuffed tenderloin. Michael tossed together a marinade, quickly took the chill off the meat, and served it over lettuce. A little Parmesan here, a little vinaigrette there, and voilà.

10 cups greens
   (romaine, red leaf,
   frisée, Bibb)
1 tablespoon finely
   chopped fresh garlic
1 roasted red bell
   pepper, peeled,
   seeded, and chopped
1 cup diced red onion
½ teaspoon granulated
   garlic
½ teaspoon Tabasco
¼ teaspoon white
   pepper
¼ teaspoon cayenne
   pepper

½ teaspoon salt
Juice of 1 lime, divided
1¼ pounds beef
   tenderloin, well
   trimmed
Vinaigrette Dressing
2 cups fresh Parmesan
   cheese, grated fine
2½ cups veal demi-
   glace or au jus
2 red peppers, roasted
   and julienned
2 gold peppers, roasted
   and julienned

Wash greens thoroughly in ice cold water, drain, and refrigerate. In food processor, combine garlic, red bell pepper, red onion, granulated garlic, Tabasco, white pepper, cayenne pepper, salt, and 1 teaspoon of lime juice. Process until smooth. Rub tenderloin with marinade, wrap in plastic, and refrigerate at least ½ hour. Grill over Southern hardwoods until rare. Wrap in plastic, and refrigerate until firm. Slice into wafer-thin slices. Toss greens with Vinaigrette Dressing. Arrange on platter. Sprinkle with Parmesan cheese. Surround with slices of smoked tenderloin. Ladle veal demi-glace around tenderloin. Garnish with red and yellow bell pepper strips and Parmesan cheese.

Vinaigrette Dressing:

½ teaspoon finely
   chopped garlic
4 tablespoons herb-
   flavored vinegar

2 teaspoons Dijon
   mustard
1 teaspoon lime juice
1 cup olive oil (extra
   virgin)

Prepare salad vinaigrette by whisking together garlic, herb-flavored vinegar, Dijon mustard and lime juice. Slowly drizzle in extra virgin olive oil while whisking continuously.

Yield: 10 servings
Michael A. Richard

Cajun Pasta Salad with Shrimp and Basil Vinaigrette

BRONZE—1985

1 pound cooked bow tie pasta
8 ounces cooked cleaned shrimp (70 to 90 count)
4 tablespoons finely minced green onions
1/2 cup diced, roasted red, yellow and green peppers
1 clove garlic, chopped
1/4 cup fresh basil chiffonade
2 eggs or 1/2 cup egg substitute
2 tablespoons Moutarde du Dijon
1/2 cup red wine vinegar
1 cup cottonseed oil
1/2 teaspoon cayenne pepper
1/2 teaspoon white pepper

Toss together the first six ingredients in a salad bowl. For the vinaigrette, whisk the two eggs in a bowl until tiny pinpoint bubbles appear in the lemony froth. Add the mustard; then incorporate the oil into the egg gradually in a thin steady stream while whisking. When half the oil has been added in this manner, add half of the vinegar and continue whisking. Add the remainder of the oil, the remainder of the vinegar, cayenne pepper, and white pepper. Toss with pasta mixture, and chill 3 hours before serving.

Yield: 12 servings
Bryan Richard

Bryan developed this recipe for a Senate luncheon hosted by John Breaux, benefitting the American Cancer Society. It was part of a "Cajun Healthy" buffet prepared in Lafayette and flown to D.C.

Balsamic, Pecan, Cane Vinaigrette Dressing

1 quart olive oil
1 cup balsamic vinegar
1/2 tablespoon thyme leaf
1/2 tablespoon basil
1/2 tablespoon oregano
1 teaspoon granulated garlic
Juice of 1 lime
1/2 cup Creole mustard
1/2 cup cane syrup
1 tablespoon Tabasco
1/2 teaspoon all-purpose seasoning
1 cup pecans
Mixed greens

Mix all ingredients in large mixing bowl. With wire whip blend until all ingredients are well incorporated. Serve over mixed greens.

Yield: 8 servings
Britt Shockley

If you can't find Creole mustard use Dijon mustard. If you can't find cane syrup use honey.

Salad Galvez

30 jumbo shrimp	1 teaspoon rosemary
2 cups peanut oil	1 teaspoon cumin
1 cup chopped green onions	Avocado Stuffing
8 garlic cloves	2 heads of lettuce or equivalent mixed greens
1 cup Lea & Perrins White Wine Worcestershire	3 carrots
4 teaspoons all-purpose seasoning	Dressing

Marinate shrimp in peanut oil and next 6 ingredients for 2 to 3 hours. Grill seasoned shrimp until tender. Cool shrimp, slice partially through, and fill with Avocado Stuffing. Lay shrimp on bed of lettuce. Grate strips of carrots on salad. Serve with dressing.

Avocado Stuffing:

4 large avocados	2 teaspoons Lea & Perrins Worcestershire
1 onion, grated	1 teaspoon garlic powder
4 teaspoons lime juice	
2 tomatoes, skinned and seeded	Salt and pepper to taste

Gently mash avocados. Blend in remaining ingredients.

Dressing:

4 teaspoons fresh lemon juice	4 teaspoons horseradish
2 teaspoons red wine vinegar	2 teaspoons all-purpose seasoning
2 teaspoons Lea & Perrins White Wine Worcestershire	2 teaspoons ketchup
	1 cup olive oil
4 teaspoons Creole mustard	1/2 cup chopped celery
	1/2 cup chopped green onion

Combine all ingredients, and blend well.

Yield: 10 servings
Joseph Schreiber C.W.C.

All-purpose seasoning is a mixture of 12 herbs and spices with a 10% salt content.

Pork Tenderloin Salad

3 (2-ounce) medallions
  of pork tenderloin
3 ounces virgin olive oil
1/8 sprig of rosemary,
  finely minced
Salt and pepper to taste
1/2 carrot, finely
  julienned
1/4 yellow bell pepper,
  julienned
1/8 red bell pepper,
  julienned
1/4 red onion, julienned
4 ounces mixed greens
2 ounces balsamic
  vinegar
3 walnuts, shelled and
  chopped
2 ounces fresh goat
  cheese

Marinate pork in olive oil for 20 minutes with fresh rosemary and salt and pepper. Remove tenderloins from marinade, and broil until done. Mix carrots and next 3 vegetables with greens. Add vinegar. Cut tenderloin into strips. Add walnuts. Garnish with goat cheese.

Yield: 2 servings
Derrick Trotter

Vidalia Onion Salad with Oranges

Red and green leaf
  lettuce
1 Vidalia onion, sliced
1 orange
1/4 cup Roquefort cheese
1/4 cup chopped walnuts
Raspberry vinegar
Olive oil

Place lettuce leaves on plate. Top with slices of Vidalia onion. Peel orange, and separate into segments; place orange segments on onion slices. Sprinkle with crumbled Roquefort cheese and walnuts. Make vinaigrette with raspberry vinegar and olive oil, and drizzle on salad.

Yield: 2 servings
Kenneth Veron

SILVER—1988

Grilled Shrimp Salad with Peaches

2 (1-pound) cans peach
  halves with syrup
5 ounces white wine
1 tablespoon parsley
1 (5-ounce) bottle Tiger
  Sauce
1 teaspoon seasoned
  salt
1 teaspoon cayenne
  pepper
1 teaspoon cumin
3 tablespoons cilantro,
  chopped

1 tablespoon oregano,
  chopped
2 pounds cleaned
  shrimp (21 to 25
  count)
Romaine lettuce
Purple cabbage,
  chopped
Fresh peach slices
Orange slices, peeled
Mangoes, sliced
Dressing

Drain canned peaches; set peaches aside. Combine 2 cups peach syrup and next 8 ingredients; mix well, and reserve ¼ cup mixture for the dressing. Marinate shrimp in marinade for one hour in refrigerator. Grill shrimp over charcoal fire with mesquite chips. Place romaine lettuce on salad plate with cabbage. Arrange shrimp with slices of fresh and canned peaches, orange slices, and mangoes. Lightly pour dressing over entire salad.

Dressing:

½ cup olive oil
¼ cup fresh lemon juice
¼ cup fresh lime juice

¼ cup peach marinade
  sauce

Blend all ingredients well; serve over salad.

Yield: 6 servings
Kenneth Veron

Vegetables

Summer Squash Mousse with Zucchini Blossom Fritter

½ cup finely diced yellow onions
½ cup finely diced red onions
2 tablespoons butter
1 teaspoon finely chopped garlic
½ teaspoon white pepper
½ teaspoon salt
½ teaspoon cayenne pepper
½ cup red bell peppers (roasted, peeled, seeded, and diced)

½ cup yellow bell peppers (roasted, peeled, seeded, and diced)
4 cups finely diced summer squash
1 tablespoon chopped fresh basil
5 eggs, lightly beaten
2 cups heavy cream
Timbale Stuffing
Zucchini Blossom Fritters

Sauté yellow and red onion in butter until slightly caramelized. Add garlic, white pepper, salt, and cayenne pepper. Toss in red and yellow peppers. Add summer squash, basil, eggs, and heavy cream. Blend in food processor until smooth. Pipe around sides of buttered timbale molds, leaving space in center for Timbale Stuffing. Stuff and cover with squash mousse. Place timbales in deep pans. Fill with hot water two-thirds up sides. Bake in preheated 350° oven about 30 minutes or until set. Let stand 5 minutes. Remove from mold. Arrange on plate w'th a red pepper coulis and a Zucchini Fritter Blossom.

Timbale Stuffing:

2 cups finely diced summer squash
1 cup finely diced shiitake mushrooms
¼ cup finely diced yellow onions
¼ cup finely diced red onions

1 tablespoon olive oil (extra virgin)
Madeira wine
Salt, white pepper, cayenne, and cracked pepper to taste

Sauté squash, mushrooms, and onions in olive oil. Deglaze with Madeira wine. Season to taste. Stuff prepared timbale molds.

(Continued on next page)

Summer Squash Mousse with Zucchini Blossom Fritter (continued)

Zucchini Fritter Blossoms:

1 egg
$^1/_2$ teaspoon granulated garlic
$^1/_4$ teaspoon granulated onion
$^1/_2$ teaspoon seasoned salt
$^1/_2$ cup milk
$^1/_2$ cup cornstarch
1 teaspoon baking powder
10 zucchini blossoms opened (cleaned)

In large bowl mix the egg, garlic, onion, seasoned salt, and milk. Sift cornstarch with baking powder. Add to egg mixture. Whisk until smooth, adjusting consistency, if necessary, by adding milk or cornstarch. Dip zucchini blossoms into batter. Fry at 360° until golden.

Yield: 10 servings
Michael A. Richard

secretsecretsecretsecretsecretsecretsecretsecretsecretsecretsecretsecretsecret
You need fresh zucchini blossoms for this winning recipe. Michael could pick fresh vegetables and herbs from a friend's garden in Cankton, Louisiana. His dining customers always loved the zucchini blossoms.

Praline Yams

2 (1-pound) cans cut yams, undrained
$^1/_2$ cup sugar
$^1/_2$ teaspoon salt
2 eggs
$^1/_2$ stick butter, melted
1 teaspoon cinnamon
$^1/_2$ teaspoon nutmeg
$^1/_2$ cup milk
2 teaspoons vanilla
$^1/_2$ cup light brown sugar
$^1/_3$ cup flour
1 cup pecans, chopped
$^1/_3$ stick butter, melted

Joe's favorite yam recipe was developed by one of Lafayette's premier gourmet chefs and bakers, Kathleen Short.

In a large mixing bowl, combine yams with a mixture of sugar, salt, eggs, $^1/_2$ stick butter, cinnamon, and nutmeg. Beat with mixer until smooth. Add milk and vanilla. Stir until mixed. Pour into greased casserole dish. For topping, combine brown sugar, flour, and pecans. Spread on top of yam mixture. Drizzle $^1/_3$ stick melted butter over top. Bake at 350° for 30 to 35 minutes until bubbly.

Yield: 12 servings
Joseph Broussard

You can do all mixing in food processor.

secretsecretsecretsecretsecretsecretsecretsecretsecretsecretsecretsecretsecret
You know you're in Cajun country with Louisiana yams and pecans.

Smothered Potatoes and Sausage

This recipe is an adaptation of another family favorite that was good enough to be the main dish or a special treat as a side dish.

1 ½ cups diced onion
½ cup diced red bell peppers
¼ cup diced green bell peppers
¼ cup diced celery
1 tablespoon chopped garlic
1 tablespoon LouAna cottonseed oil
2 links smoked sausage, sliced
6 to 8 medium potatoes, peeled and coarsely chopped

1 quart chicken stock
1 tablespoon seasoned salt
¼ teaspoon white pepper
¼ teaspoon granulated garlic
1 teaspoon granulated onion
1 teaspoon Tabasco
1 tablespoon thinly sliced green onions
1 tablespoon finely chopped parsley

In black iron Dutch oven or heavy pot, sauté onion, peppers, celery, and garlic in cottonseed oil. Add sausage; brown well over high heat, stirring and scraping pan bottom. Add potatoes. Let potatoes brown slightly; then add chicken stock, seasoned salt, white pepper, granulated garlic, granulated onion, and Tabasco. Stir potatoes to prevent sticking. Lower heat and allow to cook until tender. Additional water or stock may need to be added. Potatoes should not dissolve completely, leaving a potato gravy and potato pieces along with sausage and lots of onions. Just before serving, add green onions and parsley.

Yield: 12 servings
Michael A. Richard

This tasty dish can be a meal in itself, or serve with rice and gravy and smothered steak.

Artichoke Fruitti di Mare

BRONZE—1993

10 artichokes
24 ounces artichoke hearts
4 ounces crawfish, peeled
¾ cup heavy cream, divided
1 teaspoon crushed garlic, divided
1 teaspoon crushed basil, divided
1 teaspoon crushed oregano, divided
3 tablespoons Parmesan cheese, divided
½ teaspoon salt
8 ounces lump crabmeat
¼ cup chicken stock
½ teaspoon black pepper

Steam artichokes for 30 minutes; then remove leaves from bottom and reserve both. Place artichoke hearts, crawfish, ¼ cup heavy cream, ½ teaspoon garlic, ½ teaspoon basil, ½ teaspoon oregano, 1 teaspoon Parmesan cheese, and ½ teaspoon salt in a food processor and puree. Mix crabmeat with puree, and mold mixture around artichoke bottoms. Top with 2 tablespoons Parmesan cheese, and bake at 450° for 8 minutes. For sauce, place ½ cup heavy cream, ½ teaspoon garlic, ½ teaspoon basil, ½ teaspoon oregano, 2 teaspoons Parmesan cheese, ¼ cup chicken stock, and ½ teaspoon black pepper in a small skillet; simmer on medium heat until desired consistency is reached. Place sauce on plate, top with artichoke bottoms, and surround plate with reserved artichoke leaves.

Yield: 10 servings
Brian Blanchard

This dish makes a great dip served with club crackers.

Crunchy Corn Salsa

2 green onions, minced
2 large tomatoes, diced
1 large clove garlic, minced
½ teaspoon minced jalapeño pepper
⅓ cup canned or frozen whole-kernel corn
1 tablespoon olive oil
2 tablespoons lemon juice
½ teaspoon cumin
2 tablespoons chopped fresh cilantro

Combine all ingredients, and chill several hours.

Yield: 4 servings
Lynn Epstein, LDN, RD

This goes great with black bean soup or three-bean chili chowder.

This is about as light as you can get.

Meatless Spaghetti Sauce

1 (12-ounce) can tomatoes with juice
1 bell pepper
1 pickled jalapeño pepper
1 tablespoon jalapeño juice
2 medium-size yellow onions
3 large ribs celery
4 cloves garlic
1 (15-ounce) can tomato sauce

1 (15-ounce) can mushroom stems and pieces
3 Knorr beef bouillon cubes
1 teaspoon black pepper
2 tablespoons crushed oregano
1 tablespoon brown sugar
1 cup bran

Blend the first 7 ingredients in a food processor. Add this mixture to the remaining ingredients, except the bran, in a large pot (Dutch oven or stockpot). Cook slowly on medium heat for 1 hour. Add bran and reheat.

Yield: 6 servings
Lynn Epstein, LDN, RD

Serve on spaghetti squash or spaghetti pasta.

Use reduced-fat sour cream and cream of chicken soup. Replace butter with margarine, and reduce to only 2 tablespoons to lightly coat stuffing.

Lynn's family won't let her in the door at the holidays without this dish.

Squash Casserole

2 pounds summer squash, sliced
1 large onion, grated
1 medium carrot, grated
½ cup sour cream
1 (11-ounce) can cream of chicken soup
1 tablespoon sage

1 tablespoon poultry seasoning
½ cup butter, melted
½ pound cornbread dressing
½ pound herbed stuffing
2 tablespoons chopped fresh parsley

Cook squash and drain. In a large mixing bowl, add squash, onion, carrot, sour cream, cream of chicken soup, sage, and poultry seasoning. Mix ingredients together. In a separate mixing bowl, combine butter, cornbread dressing, herbed stuffing, and chopped parsley. Alternate layers with squash mixture and stuffing mixture in a casserole dish. Bake at 350° 30 to 35 minutes. Cover for first 20 to 25 minutes; then uncover to lightly brown the top.

Yield: 10 servings
Lynn Epstein, LDN, RD

Add a few layers of shrimp to make this a one-dish meal. For a moister casserole, sprinkle chicken broth over the top before baking.

Carrots Almondine

²/₃ cups almonds, sliced
4 cups carrots, sliced
3 tablespoons butter
¹/₂ cup honey

2 tablespoons lemon
    juice
1 teaspoon salt
¹/₂ teaspoon nutmeg
¹/₄ teaspoon garlic

Blanch almonds in 300° oven just until brown. In large skillet, sauté carrots and almonds in butter, honey, and lemon juice on low. Add seasonings, and continue cooking until carrots are nicely glazed.

Yield: 8 servings
Henry Gillett

Macque Choux

4 tablespoons butter
²/₃ cup diced onion
¹/₃ cup diced bell pepper
1 teaspoon minced
    fresh garlic
10 ounces whole-kernel
    corn
1 (14-ounce) can cream-
    style corn
1 jalapeño, deseeded
    and minced

1 medium tomato,
    peeled and diced
1 teaspoon sugar
1¹/₂ teaspoons salt
¹/₄ teaspoon cayenne
    pepper
¹/₄ teaspoon black
    pepper
1 dash Worcestershire
    sauce
¹/₂ cup whipping cream

Corn was introduced to the Cajuns by the native Indians who lived here. This became the Cajun version of the Indians' ingredient.

In a saucepan, melt butter on low fire. Add the onion, bell pepper, and garlic; sauté until onions are clear. Stir often. Add whole-kernel corn, and stir well. Cook corn until tender. Add cream-style corn, jalapeño, tomato, sugar, salt, cayenne, black pepper, and Worcestershire; stir and simmer for 2 minutes. Add whipping cream; stir and simmer for 2 additional minutes. Remove from heat. Put one-fourth of mixture in food processor and puree. Return puree to the pot, and mix well.

Yield: 4 to 6 servings
Roy Lyons

Serve with roast pork or beef.

Use butter-flavored vegetable oil instead of butter; use low-fat evaporated milk instead of cream.

This is best when using fresh sweet corn on the cob. However, by mixing above recipe you get the same flavor and texture of the fresh corn on the cob, that which has its own milk.

Chef Koval traveled the rural regions around Lafayette to find the fresh fruits of the season. He named this dish after the small farming community where he found the best eggplant.

Eggplant Crêpe Carencro

1 large eggplant	Salt to taste
2 cups peanut oil	Pepper to taste
1 cup flour	Filling
6 eggs, beaten well	Sauce

Peel eggplant, and cut from stem to bottom into $1/16$-inch slices. Heat oil in pan keeping it at a medium degree. Dredge eggplant slices in flour. Then dip eggplant slices in egg, covering both sides; let excess egg drain off. Brown both sides to a golden color. Place on paper towel to drain, and sprinkle with salt and pepper. Add filling to each slice, roll up, and secure with picks. Serve with hot sauce.

Filling:

5 tablespoons butter	1 ½ pounds fresh
1 medium-size red	spinach, rinsed well
onion, finely diced	Fresh garlic to taste
½ pound fennel, peeled	Salt to taste
and finely diced	Pepper to taste

Melt butter in pan to a golden brown color. Add onion and fennel, and cook 2 minutes. Add spinach cook until wilted. Add garlic, and season with salt and pepper to taste.

Sauce:

3 tablespoons peanut oil	2 tablespoons green chile juice
3 tablespoons finely diced shallots	2 tablespoons white vinegar
1 tablespoon finely minced garlic	1 ½ cups coconut milk
3 tablespoons chopped sweet basil leaves	1 tablespoon finely diced turmeric root
1 tablespoon ground macadamia nuts	Salt to taste
	2 teaspoons sweet basil leaves

Heat oil in saucepan; sauté shallots and garlic for 2 minutes. Add chopped basil leaves; sauté for another minute. Add macadamia nuts, and continue to sauté 2 minutes more. Pour in chile juice, vinegar, and coconut milk. Sprinkle in the turmeric, and season with salt. Bring to boil. Reduce heat, and simmer 8 minutes, stirring constantly. Pour mixture into blender, and process until smooth. Pour back into saucepan, add whole basil leaves, and serve hot.

Yield: 6 servings
Ken Koval

Stuffed Mustard Green Leaves

2 tablespoons peanut
  oil
3 tablespoons finely
  diced shallot
1 ½ teaspoons finely
  minced garlic

2 red chiles, seeded and
  finely diced
1 cup bean sprouts
Salt to taste
8 mustard green leaves,
  blanched

Heat oil in pan, sauté shallot, garlic, and chiles until light brown, about 1 to 2 minutes. Add bean sprouts, and sauté 1 minute more and season with salt. Remove from heat, flatten leaves, spread out sprout mixture into middle of each leaf. Fold leaf over the mixture, and form it into a small pouch; tie with lemon grass. Steam 1 to 2 minutes before serving.

Yield: 8 servings
Ken Koval

Corn and Zucchini Timbale

2 ½ cups fresh corn
  kernels
⅔ cup water
5 large eggs
1 tablespoon flour
1 teaspoon sugar
1 teaspoon salt

2 medium zucchini,
  peeled
1 sun-dried tomato,
  finely sliced
1 ½ teaspoons minced
  fresh thyme

Puree corn with ⅔ cup water for 1 minute. Add eggs, flour, sugar, and salt, and puree 1 more minute. Strain puree through fine sieve into bowl, pressing hard on solids. With a vegetable peeler, cut thin lengthwise slices from the zucchini, avoiding the cores; set aside. Grate enough of the remaining zucchini to make 1 cup. Squeeze the grated zucchini in a towel until dry, and then stir into corn mixture with tomato and thyme. Arrange 2 slices of zucchini in each buttered timbale mold or custard cup, and add corn mixture. Cover with aluminum foil, and bake in 350° oven in water bath for 30 to 40 minutes or until firm. Remove from oven, and let cool; unmold when cool to the touch, and serve warm.

Yield: 6 servings
Ken Koval

Cajuns love cabbage as a side dish. Roy took it a step further by making it a main course or a side dish to any meat entrée. Seafood is readily available in Acadiana, so for the Culinary Classic he tried a unique blend of flavors...it worked!

Cabbage Patch Shrimp

4 strips bacon
½ cup butter
¾ cup diced onion
1 tablespoon minced fresh garlic
1 large head of cabbage, shredded
4 ounces tomato sauce
1 tablespoon sugar
2 tablespoons butter
1 pound shrimp (70 to 90 count), cleaned
1¾ cups rich shrimp stock
½ cup diced red bell pepper

1¼ teaspoons salt
¾ teaspoon cayenne
½ teaspoon black pepper
¼ teaspoon dried thyme
1 tablespoon Tony Chachere's Creole Seasoning
¼ teaspoon Worcestershire sauce
1 teaspoon Try Me Tiger sauce
¼ teaspoon Tabasco
¾ cup thinly sliced green onion

In a black pot, sauté bacon until the fat has rendered out. Remove crisp bacon strips, and allow to cool; then crumble and put back in pot. Add ½ cup butter, and allow it to melt. Fold in the onion, garlic, cabbage, tomato sauce, and sugar; stir well. Simmer for 15 minutes. In a small skillet, melt 2 tablespoons butter; add the shrimp, and sauté just until pink. Place shrimp in the large pot. Add the shrimp stock and next 9 ingredients; Simmer for 6 minutes; then add green onions and serve.

Yield: 4 to 6 servings
Roy Lyons

Serve anytime for cabbage lovers or on holidays with a turkey or roast.

Tasso Green Beans

2 ounces butter
½ cup tasso, minced
½ cup chopped onion
¼ cup chopped bell pepper
¼ cup chopped celery

1 tablespoon minced garlic
1 teaspoon seasoning salt
1 teaspoon salt
4 pounds frozen cut green beans, thawed

Heat butter in sauté pan. Add tasso, onion, bell pepper, celery, garlic, seasoning salt, and salt. Sauté for 3 minutes. Add green beans, and simmer for 10 minutes or until beans are cooked.

Yield: 20 (3-ounce) servings
Patrick Mould C.E.C.

Acorn Squash with Apple Stuffing

1 to 2 pounds acorn or
  butternut squash
³/₄ cup butter, divided
1 cup chopped onion
¹/₂ cup chopped celery
2 cups whole wheat
  bread, cubed
¹/₄ cup parsley, minced
3 eggs, beaten

Tony Chachere's Creole
  Seasoning to taste
1 cup pecan pieces
3 apples, peeled, cored,
  and diced
¹/₄ teaspoon ground
  cinnamon
Water to moisten
  mixture

Peel squash, cut in half, remove seeds, and scrape centers, reserving pulp. Melt ¹/₄ cup butter, and grease squash. In pot melt the remaining ¹/₂ cup butter, and sauté the onion and celery until limp. Remove from heat, and add bread, parsley, eggs, and seasoning. Add pecans, apples, and cinnamon. Add water, if necessary, to moisten. Add pulp from squash, and mix well. Fill hollowed out squash, wrap in foil, and bake at 350° for 45 minutes. Cut squash in half, and serve hot.

Yield: 4 servings
William M. O'Dea C.E.C., A.A.C.

Cajun-Style Blackeyed Peas

9 cups water or beef
  stock, defatted
1 pound dried
  blackeyed peas
¹/₂ pound smoked ham
1¹/₂ cups chopped onion
1 cup chopped green
  bell pepper

¹/₂ cup chopped celery
1 bay leaf
3 teaspoons salt
³/₄ teaspoon red pepper
¹/₄ teaspoon black
  pepper
1 tablespoon fresh
  parsley, minced

Omit the ham, but you may need to add more salt.

Boil 9 cups water in a 5-quart Dutch oven over high heat. Add the peas, and cook, covered (leaving the lid slightly opened), for 10 minutes. Add the next 7 ingredients; cook, covered, for 30 minutes, stirring occasionally. Reduce the heat to a simmer; add the black pepper and parsley, and cook 20 minutes longer, stirring often. Using the back of a spoon, mash some of the peas against the inside of the pot. (This will give the mixture a creamy, gravy-like thickness). Remove the bay leaf before serving.

Yield: 8 cups
Enola Prudhomme

Cajun Stuffed Potatoes

10 small- to medium-
  size baking potatoes
½ cup butter
1 medium onion,
  chopped
1 large green bell
  pepper, chopped
1 medium-size red bell
  pepper, chopped
3 ounces tasso, diced
½ pound andouille
  sausage or smoked
  sausage, diced

1 pound small shrimp,
  cooked and chopped
½ cup butter, melted
12 ounces cream
  cheese, cubed
1 pound crabmeat,
  cleaned
Salt and pepper to taste
2 cups chopped green
  onions
½ pound Cheddar
  cheese, grated

Bill developed this while working at a hotel. He found it makes a good entrée, as well, by serving with a vegetable and salad.

Use olive oil in place of butter. Also use light cream cheese or fat-free Cheddar cheese.

Bake potatoes, and scoop out insides, reserving skins. Mash potatoes, and set aside. Melt ½ cup butter, and sauté onion and bell peppers until limp. Add tasso and andouille; cook 4 minutes. Add shrimp; cook lightly. Add ½ cup butter and cream cheese; cook until cream cheese melts. Remove from heat. Stir in crabmeat and mashed potatoes. Mix well, and add salt and pepper, if needed. If consistency is too heavy, add more melted butter. Stuff mixture back into potato skins, and top with green onions and Cheddar cheese; bake until hot.

Yield: 10 servings
William M. O'Dea C.E.C., A.A.C.

Use as an appetizer by replacing baking potatoes with small red potatoes.

secretsecretsecretsecretsecretsecretsecretsecretsecretsecretsecretsecret
Make it Cajun by using Savoies Andouille and Tasso.

Meat Stuffed Bell Pepper à la Leigh

2 quarts water
4 large bell peppers,
  red or green
1 tablespoon salt
10 slices bacon, cut
  into ½-inch-thick
  pieces
1 teaspoon margarine
1½ pounds ground
  meat
1 tablespoon minced
  celery
½ cup chopped red
  onion
½ cup chopped yellow
  onion
½ cup chopped green
  bell pepper
1 tablespoon salt
1 teaspoon ground
  white pepper
¼ teaspoon jalapeño
  peppers, minced
1 cup cream of chicken
  soup
1 cup cream of
  mushroom soup
1¼ cups breadcrumbs
¾ cup shredded
  Cheddar cheese

In a 3-quart pot, boil 2 quarts water. Remove caps or stems from bell pepper, and place peppers in boiling water with 1 tablespoon salt for 10 minutes. Remove from water, drain, and place in ice water to cool. Remove from ice water, and place in refrigerator until ready to stuff. In a medium skillet on high heat, cook bacon for 10 minutes. Drain; set aside. In a medium pot on high heat, melt 1 teaspoon margarine. Add ground meat, and cook for 10 minutes or until browned. Drain any extra grease from meat. Add celery, red and yellow onion, chopped bell pepper, salt, white pepper, and jalapeño; cook for 7 minutes. Add chicken soup, mushroom soup, breadcrumbs, reserved bacon, and Cheddar cheese; stir well. Cook for 3 minutes. Remove from heat, let cool for 20 minutes, and then stuff the bell peppers. Place bell peppers in a 9x12-inch baking dish. Place in 350° oven, and bake for 20 minutes.

Yield: 4 servings
Chris Oncale

Corn Maque Choux

4 cups sweet corn	1 cup milk
¼ cup oil	1 cup half-and-half
1 medium onion, chopped	3 tablespoons sugar
½ cup chopped green bell pepper	1½ teaspoons salt
½ cup chopped red bell pepper	¼ teaspoon red pepper
	½ cup chopped green onion

Using a sharp knife, cut the top of the kernels from the cob; then cut a second time. Scrape the remaining kernels from the cob with the side of the knife; set aside. Place a 5-quart Dutch oven over high heat; add the oil, onion, and bell peppers. Cook and stir 10 minutes or until onions are transparent. Reduce the heat to medium; add the corn, milk, half-and-half, sugar, salt, and red pepper. Cook and stir 10 minutes until corn is tender. Add the green onions; remove from heat, and let stand, covered, 5 minutes before serving.

Yield: 4 servings
Enola Prudhomme

Serve over hot cooked rice for main meal or a side dish.

Use vegetable cooking spray instead of oil and evaporated skimmed milk instead of cream; this will save about 30 grams of fat.

secretsecretsecretsecretsecretsecretsecretsecretsecretsecretsecretsecretsecret

This dish has been prepared in Cajun homes for many years. Enola serves it in her restaurant with sautéed crawfish or shrimp.

Fried Eggplant Rounds with Tasso Cream Sauce

¹/₄ teaspoon salt	1 cup milk
¹/₄ teaspoon red pepper	1 egg
¹/₄ teaspoon black pepper	1 cup vegetable oil
1 large eggplant, peeled and cut into 1-inch rounds	1 cup all-purpose flour
	1 cup breadcrumbs
	Cream Sauce

In a small bowl combine the salt, red pepper, and black pepper; mix well, and sprinkle over both sides of eggplant rounds; set aside. In a medium bowl, beat together milk and egg; set aside. Heat the oil in a heavy skillet over high heat until very hot. Dredge each eggplant in the flour, then dip into the milk and egg mixture, then dredge through breadcrumbs. Carefully drop each eggplant round in the hot oil, and fry about 3 minutes or until golden brown. Remove from heat, and place eggplants on a paper towel to drain; set aside and keep warm. Prepare Cream Sauce. To serve, place eggplants onto a plate, and top with the sauce. Serve hot.

Cream Sauce:

1 tablespoon butter	¹/₄ teaspoon red pepper
1 cup fresh mushrooms, thinly sliced	1 cup heavy whipping cream
¹/₂ cup tasso, minced	¹/₄ cup finely chopped green onions
¹/₄ teaspoon salt	
¹/₄ teaspoon white pepper	

Melt butter in a heavy skillet over high heat. Add the mushrooms, tasso, salt, and peppers. Cook and stir 5 minutes. Add the cream; cook and stir 5 minutes. Add the green onions, and cook and stir an additional 2 minutes or until sauce thickens.

Yield: 4 servings
Enola Prudhomme

To lighten, bake or broil eggplant rounds. For the sauce, use 8 ounces of 1% low-fat cottage cheese blended with 1 (12-ounce) can evaporated skimmed milk. You will save about 30 to 40 fat grams.

BRONZE—1992

Basket of Eggplant with Tomato Cream Sauce

1 cup butter	Garlic to taste
2 pounds eggplant, cooked, peeled, and diced	Black pepper to taste
	Salt to taste
	1 cup shredded Cheddar cheese
1 small onion, diced	
1 small bell pepper, diced	1 cup shredded jalapeño cheese
½ pound ground beef, cooked	1 eggplant
	Buttermilk
1 small tomato, diced	Seasoned flour
1 cup sour cream	Tomato Cream Sauce

Melt butter, and sauté eggplant until tender. Add onion and bell pepper. Cook until tender. Add cooked ground beef, tomato, sour cream, seasonings, and cheeses. Adjust for taste. For eggplant basket, peel an eggplant. Hollow out center until walls are about ¼ inch thick. Dip into buttermilk. Roll in seasoned flour. Deep fry until golden brown. Place eggplant mixture in basket, and serve on top of Tomato Cream Sauce.

Tomato Cream Sauce:

3 teaspoons butter	1 teaspoon tomato paste
2 teaspoons flour	
4 ounces chicken stock	Oregano to taste
8 ounces heavy cream	Salt to taste
	Pepper to taste

For sauce, melt butter and add flour. Cook until blond roux forms. Add stock, heavy cream, and tomato paste. Add seasonings. Adjust. Cook until thickened. Add sauce to individual plates.

Yield: 10 servings
Britt Shockley

Hot Shot Hashbrowns

½ pound bacon, diced	Red pepper to taste
1 onion, diced	Black pepper to taste
1 bell pepper, diced	Salt to taste
1 (3-pound) package diced hashbrowns	Granulated garlic to taste
½ cup mayonnaise	1 pound Cheddar cheese, shredded
1 (11-ounce) can cream of mushroom soup	

Sauté bacon until crisp. Remove from fat, and sauté onion and bell pepper until tender. Place hashbrowns in large bowl, and add remaining ingredients, except cheese. Place in casserole dish, and top with cheese. Cook at 350° until cheese starts to bubble.

Yield: 10 servings
Britt Shockley

This was a favorite dish at dinner parties for the United States Thunderbird Team, with which Britt's father flew. The recipe was given to his mother by a retired general of the USAF. Britt has since made it a Cajun dish.

Cornucopia of Squash

5 yellow squash
1 onion, chopped
2 large tomatoes,
  chopped
2 ounces ground beef
½ cup butter
2 ounces crabmeat
½ pound Monterey Jack
  cheese
⅛ cup jalapeños,
  chopped

Granulated garlic to
  taste
Red pepper to taste
Black pepper to taste
Salt to taste
½ cup Creole mustard
2 cups seasoned
  breadcrumbs
Herb Tomato Sauce

Hollow out squash, leaving shell intact. Sauté onion, squash pulp, tomato, and ground beef in butter until tender. Add crabmeat, cheese, peppers, and seasonings to taste. Place stuffing into squash shells. Roll in mustard then coat with breadcrumbs. Bake at 350° for 30 minutes or until center is hot. Remove from oven. Slice squash into rounds. Place on top of Herb Tomato Sauce.

Herb Tomato Sauce:
¼ pound butter
1½ tablespoons flour
1 cup chicken stock
½ cup heavy cream
½ cup tomato sauce
Basil to taste

Oregano to taste
Thyme to taste
Garlic to taste
Salt to taste
Pepper to taste

Melt butter, and add flour, stirring until blond roux forms. Add chicken stock, heavy cream and tomato sauce. Add seasonings to taste. Cook until sauce thickens.

Yield: 4 servings
Britt Shockley

Vermilion Pirogue with Shrimp and Lump Crabmeat

5 medium eggplant, peeled
1 cup all-purpose flour
1 ½ cups egg wash (2 eggs and 1 cup milk)
1 cup Progresso breadcrumbs
3 cups heavy whipping cream
1 tablespoon grated Parmesan cheese
1 teaspoon chopped garlic
½ teaspoon salt
1 teaspoon white pepper
1 pound shrimp (70 to 90 count)
½ pound lump crabmeat
2 ounces brandy
1 ½ tablespoons paprika
Vegetable oil for frying

Halve eggplants, and carve out pulp with spoon, leaving a ¼-inch shell. Batter eggplant shells with flour, egg wash, and breadcrumbs — separately and in that order. Set aside. Bring whipping cream to a boil in a large saucepan. Whisk in Parmesan cheese, garlic, salt, and white pepper. Simmer 5 minutes. Add shrimp, crabmeat, brandy, and paprika; simmer an additional 3 minutes. While sauce is simmering, fry eggplant until golden brown. Pour brandy cream sauce into cavity of fried eggplant halves, and serve immediately.

Yield: 10 servings
Chris Sogga

Panier de Legumes

2 large yellow bell
  peppers
3 large russet white
  potato, finely sliced
Salt and pepper to
  taste
1 pound fresh broccoli,
  washed and coarsely
  chopped

1 medium head
  cauliflower, separated
  into flowerets
1 medium bunch
  asparagus, sliced
1 small can baby
  carrots, drained
1 small can baby corn,
  drained
½ cup butter
Salt and pepper to taste

Grill bell peppers with hickory chips. Puree and set aside. Season potatoes, and deep fry in Bird Nest Maker to form a basket. Sauté remaining vegetables in butter; season and arrange in basket. Pour pureed bell pepper over the vegetables.

Yield: 10 servings
Jerry Sonnier C.W.C.

Fried Softshell Crawfish with Rotel Tomato Cream Sauce

3 pints heavy whipping cream
3 tablespoons fresh basil, chopped
3 tablespoons minced garlic
1 tablespoon all-purpose seasoning
4 tablespoons Rotel tomatoes, chopped
2 teaspoons Tabasco
20 softshell crawfish
2 eggs
½ cup milk
½ cup buttermilk
3 cups all-purpose flour
2 tablespoon all-purpose seasoning, divided
3 cups corn flour
Oil for frying
6 tablespoons chopped green onions
3 tablespoons minced parsley

Combine first six ingredients. Reduce till creamy; keep warm. Clean crawfish, and remove the eyes and calcium deposits; set aside. Whip eggs, milk, and buttermilk together. Mix regular flour and 1 tablespoon seasoning. Dredge crawfish in seasoned flour. Dip in milk mixture, and then dredge in corn flour seasoned with remaining 1 tablespoon seasoning. Heat oil to 350°. Drop battered crawfish in hot oil, and fry until golden brown. Add green onions and parsley to the cream sauce. Serve crawfish on a bed of sauce.

Yield: 10 servings
Patrick Mould C.E.C.

Cajun-Italian Crawfish and Mirliton Pirogue

BRONZE—1985

6 mirlitons, blanched,
  peeled, seeded
Salt and pepper to
  taste
1 pound Louisiana
  crawfish
Freshly cracked black
  pepper to taste

1 cup commercial
  Italian Olive Salad Mix
2 pounds tricolored
  tortellinis, cooked and
  cooled
Red leaf lettuce leaves

Shape the mirlitons into pirogues (diamond-shaped Cajun boats). Salt and pepper them; then refrigerate until later assembly. Place crawfish in a large glass bowl, and season with freshly cracked black pepper. Add olive salad mix, and chill thoroughly (3 to 4 hours). Combine crawfish mixture with the tortellinis. Arrange lettuce leaves on a serving platter. Place mirliton "boats" on the lettuce, and fill each with the pasta salad.

Yield: 6 servings
Bryan Richard

Garnish with deviled eggs flavored with ground ham and jalapeño brine (the liquid from the pepper jar). Serve with breadsticks.

secretsecretsecretsecretsecretsecretsecretsecretsecretsecretsecretsecretsecret
Use only fresh Louisiana crawfish, which are cooked during processing and can be used as is for cocktails or salads. Do not substitute Chinese crawfish or frozen product for this recipe. The longer you allow the salad to marinate, the better it becomes.

Crawfish and Pasta

1 onion, chopped
4 single stalks of
  celery, chopped
1 bell pepper, chopped
½ cup butter
2 pounds crawfish
1 bunch of onion tops,
  finely chopped
1 teaspoon salt

1 to 1½ teaspoons
  crushed red pepper
1 teaspoon Tabasco hot
  sauce
2 cups water
½ cup blond roux
1 (12-ounce) package
  fettuccini

Sauté onion, celery, and bell pepper in butter in stockpot. Cook until vegetables are tender. Add crawfish, onion tops, all seasonings, and 2 cups of water. Let mixture come to a boil; then add roux to thicken. Boil pasta in a separate pot until tender; mix with other ingredients or serve mixture on top of pasta.

Yield: 6 servings
Michael Chaisson C.W.C.

Singing Crawfish

This is an easy dish that Bryan once cooked tableside. It can also be made with shrimp. Serve it under a glass dome if you have one.

🪶 **Change the butter to olive oil and the cream to half-and-half.**

1 French shallot, finely minced
½ cup butter
¼ cup chopped green onions, divided
2 pounds Louisiana crawfish, with fat
1 pound fresh shiitake mushrooms, sliced
¼ cup Harvey's Bristol Cream Sherry
2 cloves elephant garlic, finely minced
2 tablespoons whole green peppercorns
Zest of 1 lemon, finely grated
½ cup heavy cream
Sea salt to taste
⅛ cup chopped fresh chives
8 to 10 dashes red Tabasco

Sauté shallot in butter in a heavy skillet briefly with ⅛ cup of the green onions. Stir in the crawfish, and simmer at least 8 minutes. Add the mushrooms, and cook until they achieve transparency. Add the sherry, garlic, peppercorns, and zest. Stir in the heavy cream, and reduce the sauce until thickened. Add sea salt to taste, the remaining green onions, chives, and Tabasco.

Yield: 6 servings
Bryan Richard

Serve over toast points or sourdough garlic croutons.

Crawfish Fettuccini

🪶 **Use fat-free cheese and regular skim milk. Add 2 to 4 tablespoons flour to replace volume lost from fat reduction.**

1 onion, chopped
1 green bell pepper, chopped
2 celery ribs, chopped
2 cloves garlic, minced
½ cup margarine
½ cup all-purpose flour
2 cups evaporated skimmed milk
2 pounds crawfish tail meat
1 (15-ounce) can mushroom stems and pieces
1 pound reduced-fat sharp Cheddar cheese, shredded
½ cup fresh parsley, chopped
1 pound fettuccini noodles, cooked

Sauté first four ingredients in margarine until onions are translucent. Add flour, and stir for approximately 5 minutes to make a white roux. Add milk, and lightly simmer approximately 5 to 10 minutes, stirring often. Add crawfish, mushrooms, and cheese, and cook on medium-low heat approximately 10 minutes. Stir occasionally. Toss parsley into mixture; then toss mixture into cooked fettuccini noodles.

Yield: 6 servings
Lynn Epstein L.D.N., R.D.

Serve with tossed salad and steamed basil zucchini.

Crawfish and Tasso Stuffed Bell Peppers

2 large onions, minced
1 bell pepper, minced
1 cup celery, chopped
2 cloves garlic,
  chopped
3/4 cup butter
1 tablespoon parsley
1 pound crawfish,
  chopped

1/4 pound tasso,
  chopped
10 slices bread, toasted
  and crumbled
1 1/2 teaspoons salt
1/2 teaspoon Tabasco
1 egg
5 medium-size bell
  peppers, seeded and
  halved

In a large skillet, sauté onion, bell pepper, celery, and garlic in butter until light brown. Stir in parsley, crawfish, tasso, and bread. Add salt and Tabasco, and blend well. Remove from heat; add egg and blend. Cook bell pepper halves in boiling, salted water about 5 minutes; then drain. Pile crawfish mixture in pepper shells, and bake at 350° for 15 to 20 minutes.

Yield: 10 servings
Joseph Broussard

Smithfield ham may be substituted for tasso. Shrimp may be substituted for crawfish.

secretsecretsecretsecretsecretsecretsecretsecretsecretsecretsecretsecret

Crawfish and tasso make this dish Cajun.

This recipe is from Joe's wife's family. It is typical fare, and was used (without tasso) on meatless Fridays in Catholic South Louisiana.

Crawfish Étouffée

This is a recipe passed down from an old Cajun chef who works in his kitchen. James made a few adjustments and has since won 6 medals and the 1994 world championship. Sharing this recipe is the hardest thing James has ever done.

1½ **cups butter, divided**
⅓ **cup flour**
2 **small onions, finely diced**
⅓ **cup finely diced bell pepper**
¾ **cup finely diced celery**
¼ **cup chopped green onion bottoms**
2 **tablespoons paprika**
1 **teaspoon cayenne pepper**
1 **teaspoon black pepper**
¾ **teaspoon garlic**
3 **tablespoons chicken bouillon**
1 **quart water**
2 **pounds crawfish tails**
½ **cup chopped green onion tops**
2 **tablespoons chopped fresh parsley**

Combine ½ cup butter and ⅓ cup flour in a small saucepan. Stir while cooking for 3 minutes over medium-high heat; remove from heat, cover, and set aside. In a 4-quart saucepan, add ½ cup butter, onion, bell pepper, celery, and green onion bottoms; cook over medium heat while stirring for 8 minutes. Add paprika, peppers, garlic, and chicken bouillon. Cook 2 more minutes while stirring. Add 1 quart water, and bring to a boil for 5 minutes. Add reserved roux, stirring well with wire whip. Reduce heat to medium, and boil for 3 minutes. Add crawfish, onion tops, and parsley; then stir in last ½ cup butter. Turn heat to low until ready to serve.

Yield: 12 servings
James Graham

Crawfish and Tasso Stuffed Mirlitons

4 mirlitons, halved
2 tablespoons butter
1 cup chopped onions
1/2 cup chopped green
  or yellow bell pepper
1 pound crawfish tails,
  peeled
1/4 cup tasso, julienned
Salt to taste

Red pepper to taste
1 egg
2 cups seasoned
  breadcrumbs, divided
2 tablespoons chopped
  green onions
2 tablespoons chopped
  parsley

Boil mirlitons in lightly salted water until tender, approximately 30 minutes. Remove from water, and cool. When cooled, remove seeds and scoop out pulp, leaving shell about 1/2 inch thick. Sauté pulp in butter with onions and bell pepper for about 10 minutes. Add crawfish and tasso, and cook for 5 minutes. Season with salt and red pepper to taste. Add egg, and stir well. Add 1 cup of breadcrumbs, and mix well. Stuff mirliton shells with crawfish mixture, and top with remaining breadcrumbs, green onions, and parsley. Bake 20 minutes at 325°.

Yield: 8 servings
William Menard

secretsecretsecretsecretsecretsecretsecretsecretsecretsecretsecretsecret

Typical Cajun flavors come alive when married in this dish. Another name for mirliton is vegetable pear or chayote. If these are not available in your area, try squash or eggplant.

America stuffs chicken with everything under the sun. Louisianans are no exception, but it's not fair because they have crawfish boudin.

Bouquet de Poulet et Ecrevisses

¹/₄ cup unsalted butter
¹/₂ cup diced sweet Vidalia onion
¹/₂ cup chopped green onion tops
¹/₄ cup chopped fresh parsley
2 teaspoons salt
1 teaspoon cayenne pepper
³/₄ teaspoon white pepper
2 teaspoons garlic powder
3 cups crawfish tails, coarsely ground
3 cups cooked rice

5 (8-ounce) chicken breasts, pounded to ¹/₄ inch thick
2 red Hungarian bell peppers, julienned
1 pound oak-smoked tasso, julienned
5 ounces poached shrimp (90 count)
6 ounces Monterey Jack, shredded
4 ounces Colby cheese, shredded
5 spears jumbo asparagus
Crawfish au Gratin Jumonville Sauce

In a cast-iron skillet, melt butter, and sauté Vidalia onion until tender. Add green onions, parsley, salt, peppers, and garlic powder, and sauté for 1 minute. Add crawfish, and cook for 3 minutes. Stir in hot cooked rice to make boudin. Take one-third boudin mixture, and mash well. Mix gently with remaining two-thirds, and refrigerate. Lay pounded, salted chicken breasts on a clean surface. Top each with a ¹/₄-inch layer of boudin. Over the boudin, lay out a row of peppers then a row of tasso then shrimp; continue this process until a ¹/₂-inch border remains at the top of each chicken breast. Sprinkle each breast with ¹/₄ cup of each cheese. At the bottom of each breast, place a spear of asparagus. With the asparagus at the tip of your fingers, roll the breast tightly, and secure with toothpicks. Poach each breast in 1 inch Jumonville Sauce at 325° for 16 minutes. Remove chicken from the sauce, and cool for 10 minutes prior to slicing. Stir juices, butter, and flavors that leaked from the chicken into the Jumonville Sauce. Ladle 2 ounces sauce onto each warm serving plate. Place 3 to 4 slices on each, and finish with steamed asparagus and dirty rice.

Crawfish au Gratin Jumonville Sauce:
¹/₄ cup butter, clarified
24 live crawfish
¹/₄ cup sliced green onion bottoms
¹/₄ cup brandy
1 quart heavy cream
1 teaspoon cayenne pepper

¹/₄ teaspoon garlic powder
¹/₄ cup butter
¹/₄ cup flour
1 ounce freshly grated Parmesan cheese
2 ounces Monterey Jack cheese, shredded

(Continued on next page)

Bouquet de Poulet et Ecrevisses (continued)

In a heavy saucepan over medium high heat, combine clarified butter and crawfish; sauté for 3 minutes. Add green onions, and continue to sauté for 5 minutes. Deglaze pan with brandy. (Be careful because the brandy will flame up.) Remove the pan from the heat, and mash the crawfish with a heavy potato masher, crushing the shells well. Return pan to stove, and add heavy cream, and reduce by one-fourth. Add cayenne and garlic powder, and continue to boil for 3 minutes. Remove sauce from heat, and strain out all solids, carefully squeezing all fat and juices from the crawfish (use a cheesecloth). Return sauce to the stove, and bring to boil. Thicken with roux made from ¼ cup butter and ¼ cup flour. Whisk continuously. Remove from heat, and stir in cheeses.

Yield: 10 servings
James Graham

Crawfish Pies

4 cups plus 2 tablespoons all-purpose flour
½ teaspoon salt
2 cups margarine
6 tablespoons ice water
½ cup butter
¼ cup finely diced onion
3 tablespoons chopped parsley
⅓ cup green onion tops

10 ounces crawfish tail meat
½ cup seafood stock
1 teaspoon cayenne pepper
½ teaspoon black pepper
1 teaspoon salt
1 teaspoon paprika
2 tablespoons flour
1½ cups cooked rice
1 egg
3 tablespoons milk

Jambalaya... Crawfish Pie...and Filé Gumbo...are the 3 most famous dishes in Louisiana. This recipe, like the music, will make you sing in the kitchen.

In a large bowl, combine sifted flour and salt. Add margarine, and mix for 30 seconds on low speed. Slowly mix in ice water until incorporated. Set aside. Roll out dough ⅛ inch thick. Cut with a 5-inch round cutter into dough rounds; set aside. In a shallow saucepan, melt ½ cup butter. Add onion, parsley, and onion tops; cook for 10 minutes. Add crawfish, and cook for 3 more minutes. Add seafood stock and seasonings; gradually stir in flour. Cook for 3 minutes. Stir in rice, and cover; Cook for 5 minutes. Fill center of each dough circle with 3 ounces of filling. Fold over and brush with mixture of egg and milk; then crimp with fork. Deep fry at 360° for 3 minutes.

Yield: 12 servings
James Graham

Crawfish Tasso Sauté

2 tablespoons oil
2 tablespoons minced
  onion
1 tablespoon minced
  bell pepper
1 tablespoon minced
  celery
1 large mushroom,
  sliced
1/2 teaspoon seasoning
  salt
1/4 teaspoon Tabasco

2 ounces tasso,
  chopped
1 teaspoon chopped
  garlic
3 ounces crawfish tails
2 tablespoon shrimp
  stock
1 tablespoon white wine
1 tablespoon chopped
  green onion
1 tablespoon chopped
  parsley
1 tablespoon butter

Heat oil over high heat in sauté pan. Sauté onion and next six ingredients until clear, browning slightly. Add garlic and next three ingredients; cook until liquid is almost reduced and crawfish are hot. Add green onion, parsley, and butter. Heating until butter melts.

Yield: 2 servings
Patrick Mould C.E.C.

Serve with seasoned rice or buttered pasta.

Crawfish-Stuffed Filet Mignon

3 gallons veal stock
1 bottle port
1/2 bottle brandy
2 (8-ounce) filet mignon
2 cups whipped butter
1 tablespoon fresh dill
1 tablespoon fresh basil
1 teaspoon fresh thyme

1 tablespoon green
  onion
1 teaspoon salt
1 teaspoon cayenne
  pepper
8 ounces fresh crawfish
  tails

Cook veal stock for 4 hours. Add port and brandy. Reduce sauce until thickened (approximately 1/2 gallon); keep warm. Cut pocket on side of filets, about halfway through; set aside. Stir together whipped butter and next 7 ingredients for the stuffing. Fill filets with stuffing. Grill. Pour sauce over grilled stuffed filets, and serve.

Yield: 2 servings
Chris Sogga

Crawfish Capellini

1 pound angel hair
  pasta
1 cup diced onion
½ cup diced celery
½ cup diced green bell
  pepper
½ cup diced red bell
  pepper
1 teaspoon fennel
  seeds
2 tablespoons chopped
  garlic

½ pound butter or
  margarine
1 pound Louisiana
  crawfish tails
1 tablespoon chopped
  fresh basil
1 teaspoon Tony
  Chachere's seasoned
  salt
1 teaspoon Tabasco
2 cups heavy cream
1 cup freshly grated
  Parmesan cheese

Substitute
half-and-half for
the heavy cream.
Eliminate butter
and use a
nonstick pan and
vegetable
cooking spray.

Prepare angel hair pasta according to package directions; set aside. In large pan, sauté onion, celery, bell peppers, and fennel seeds until onions just begin to caramelize. Add garlic toward the end. Add butter, crawfish tails, basil, seasoned salt, and Tabasco. Sauté until heated throughout. Add heavy cream, and cook over medium to high heat until cream comes to a boil. Add pasta. Cook to desired consistency. Add Parmesan cheese. Thickness can be adjusted by adding more or less cream and by varying the cooking time.

Yield: 6 servings
Michael A. Richard

Serve on a warm plate, and sprinkle with Parmesan. You can garnish it with fried soft-shell crawfish and curly parsley.

This recipe combines traditional Cajun spices with fennel as a new twist for the ever-popular angel hair pasta.

Crawfish and Cheese Puffs

½ cup finely diced
onion
¼ cup finely diced red
bell pepper
1 tablespoon butter
½ pound crawfish tails
¼ teaspoon granulated
onion
¼ teaspoon granulated
garlic

½ teaspoon Tabasco
4 ounces hot pepper
cheese, grated
2 ounces golden velvet
cheese, grated
2 ounces cream cheese
3 to 4 sheets puff
pastry

Sauté onion and pepper in 1 tablespoon butter until softened. Add crawfish tails. Stir and warm thoroughly. Season with granulated onion, garlic, and Tabasco. Add pepper cheese, golden velvet, and cream cheese; mix thoroughly. Let cool. Cut out puff pastry circles using a 3-inch scalloped round pastry cutter and a 2½-inch plain round cutter. Place 1 tablespoon of crawfish cheese mixture in center of 1- to 3-inch scalloped circle. Cover with a 2½-inch circle. Crimp around edges to seal. Bake at 400° for approximately 12 to 15 minutes until golden brown.

Yield: 12 servings
Michael A. Richard

Puffs can be laced with Mornay sauce. Because puff pastry dries out so quickly, you can cut dough in squares and wrap up like Chinese dumplings.

secretsecretsecretsecretsecretsecretsecretsecretsecretsecretsecretsecret

The combination of crawfish and cheese makes one think he is in heaven. Crawfish done correctly any which way is awesome.

Crawfish Étouffée

½ cup butter
1 large onion, diced
1 large bell pepper, diced
1½ tablespoons all-purpose flour
1½ cups seafood stock
¼ teaspoon salt
⅛ teaspoon red pepper
⅛ teaspoon white pepper

⅛ teaspoon black pepper
⅛ teaspoon garlic
½ teaspoon paprika
1 pound crawfish tails
1 cup soft butter
¼ cup sliced green onions
¼ cup chopped parsley
Steamed rice

This recipe is the 1991, 1992, and 1993 world championship crawfish étouffée recipe.

Melt ½ cup butter over medium high heat in heavy-bottomed saucepan. Add onion and bell pepper; cook until soft. Add flour, and stir well to blend. Cook 5 minutes. Add seafood stock, and whisk until smooth. Add seasonings. Bring to boil; then simmer 30 minutes. Add crawfish tails. Blend well, and cook 10 minutes. Lower heat, whip in soft butter until incorporated (do not bring to a boil). Add green onions and parsley. Serve over steamed rice.

Yield: 4 servings
Britt Shockley

Shrimp or crabmeat may be substituted.

Fried Softshell Crawfish with Acadiana Sauce

10 softshell crawfish
1 cup buttermilk
1 teaspoon red pepper
2 cups heavy whipping cream
1 tablespoon Parmesan cheese
1 teaspoon chopped garlic

½ teaspoon salt
1 teaspoon white pepper
1 tablespoon Cajun Power garlic sauce
3 dashes Tabasco
1 cup all-purpose flour
Vegetable oil for frying

Remove face of crawfish with scissors. Marinate crawfish in buttermilk and red pepper for 1 hour. For Acadiana Sauce, bring whipping cream to a boil in a large saucepan. Whisk in Parmesan cheese, garlic, salt, white pepper, garlic sauce, and Tabasco. Simmer 5 minutes. Remove crawfish from marinade, and batter with flour. Deep fry until golden brown. Layer sauce on round salad plate with crawfish arranged on sauce.

Yield: 10 servings
Chris Sogga

Andouille, Artichoke, Crawfish Bisque

½ cup butter
1 large red bell pepper, julienned
1 large yellow bell pepper, julienned
1 large green bell pepper, julienne
1 large yellow onion, julienned
1 (16-ounce) can artichoke hearts, chopped
1 pound andouille sausage, diced
3 tablespoons flour
1 cup dry Vermouth
1 cup hot chicken stock
1 cup half-and-half
2 cups heavy whipping cream
¼ teaspoon cayenne pepper
¼ teaspoon black pepper
½ teaspoon oregano
Salt to taste
1 pound crawfish tails
1 cup jalapeño cheese, shredded
Parsley

Melt butter. Sauté vegetables and andouille sausage until vegetables are tender and sausage lightly browned. Add flour, and cook for 5 to 8 minutes until blond roux forms. Add Vermouth, hot chicken stock, half-and-half, and heavy cream. Add cayenne and black peppers, oregano, and salt. Cook until thickened. Add crawfish. Adjust seasonings to taste. Garnish with cheese and parsley.

Yield: 10 servings
Britt Shockley

secretsecretsecretsecretsecretsecretsecretsecretsecretsecretsecretsecret
Andouille sausage makes this dish extra tasty.

Seafood

GOLD 1984

Oysters Rouge et Vert

1 box rock salt	Rouge Topping
36 oysters	Vert Topping
36 oyster shells	Sauce Hollandaise

Cover baking sheet with rock salt. Place an oyster and a bit of the oyster liquor on each oyster shell. Put a heaping teaspoonful of the rouge topping on one end of the oyster covering to the edge of the shell, and a teaspoon full of Vert Topping on the other end. Place the oysters on the rock salt, and bake in a 400° oven for 12 minutes. Remove from oven. Place a teaspoon full of the Hollandaise in the middle of each oyster, dividing rouge and vert, and serve.

Rouge Topping:

3 ripe red bell peppers	4 ounces mushrooms
2 tablespoons olive oil	2 tablespoons butter
8 ounces fresh sausage	2 tablespoons parsley, minced
1 cup fresh breadcrumbs (from French bread)	Salt and black pepper

Clean bell peppers, slice, put in a heavy covered saucepan with 2 tablespoons olive oil, and let cook covered over very low heat for 45 minutes. The peppers should be very soft. Drain for 10 minutes in a colander; then puree in a food processor, and set aside. Cook and crumble the sausage in a skillet. Drain thoroughly. Degrease further with paper towels. Slice mushrooms, and sauté quickly in butter. Combine red pepper puree, sausage, breadcrumbs, mushrooms, and parsley. Season to taste with salt and black pepper.

Vert Topping:

2 pounds fresh spinach	½ cup heavy cream
1 cup boiled, spiced shrimp, peeled	½ cup milk
3 tablespoons butter	Salt to taste
3 tablespoons all-purpose flour	White pepper to taste
	Red pepper to taste
	Nutmeg to taste

Cook the spinach, and drain thoroughly, squeezing out excess water. Chop the shrimp into small pieces. Make béchamel sauce by melting the butter in a saucepan. Add flour, and cook over medium heat for 2 minutes. Remove from heat, and let sit until the mixture stops bubbling. Slowly beat in cream and milk with a wire whisk, beating until smooth. Return to heat and cook, stirring constantly until sauce thickens and comes to a boil. Season to taste

(Continued on next page)

Oysters Rouge et Vert (continued)

with salt, white pepper, red pepper, and nutmeg. Combine spinach, shrimp and enough sauce to hold the mixture together. Correct seasoning.

Sauce Hollandaise:

3 egg yolks	1 cup butter, melted
1 tablespoon lemon juice	Red pepper to taste
	Salt (optional)

Beat egg yolks with a wire whisk until sticky and lemon colored. Beat in lemon juice. Over barely simmering water or a low flame, cook the egg yolks, stirring constantly until slightly thickened. Be very careful not to curdle them. Remove from heat, beat in drop by drop, the hot melted butter to achieve a thick hollandaise. Season to taste with red pepper and salt, if needed.

Yield: 8 entrées or 12 appetizers
Joseph Broussard

secretsecretsecretsecretsecretsecretsecretsecretsecretsecretsecretsecret

The combination of the ethnic flavor derived from blending the roasted peppers and smoky Cajun sausage in the Rouge and the traditional Florentine in the Vert tied together with a good Hollandaise makes this a real Cajun Culinary Classic.

Shrimp Imonelli

 BRONZE—1990

¼ pound butter	1 tablespoon cracked black pepper
3 pounds cleaned shrimp	1 tablespoon ground nutmeg
1 tablespoon salt	1 cup white wine
1 tablespoon crushed garlic	½ cup heavy whipping cream
1 tablespoon crushed oregano	2 tablespoons Parmesan cheese
1 tablespoon crushed basil	

Place butter in skillet; melt over medium heat. Add shrimp, and sauté for about 4 minutes. Then add salt, garlic, oregano, basil, black pepper, nutmeg, and white wine. Bring to a boil for 2 or 3 minutes; then remove from heat. Strain contents, and remove shrimp. Put liquid in skillet; add cream and Parmesan cheese, and bring to a boil. Add shrimp, and let simmer for about 5 minutes.

Yield: 10 servings
Brian J. Blanchard

SILVER—1983

Substitute skim milk or no-fat sour cream for heavy cream. Replace butter with vegetable oil.

Oysters Broussard

36 unshucked oysters
3 cloves garlic, minced
1 cup canned tomatoes, drained and pureed
1/2 cup dry breadcrumbs
2 (81/2-ounce) cans artichoke hearts, drained and pureed
1 cup whipping cream
1/4 cup finely chopped celery
1 to 11/4 teaspoons salt
Dash of cayenne
1/2 pound crabmeat
1/2 pound mushrooms, finely chopped
3 tablespoons melted butter or margarine
1/2 cup minced green onions
1/4 cup chopped parsley
1/2 pound ham, finely cubed
1/4 cup sherry
1 cup Parmesan cheese (grated)
Lemon wedges

Scrub oysters thoroughly in cold water. Shuck oysters, reserving liquid in deep half of shells; gently place oysters in colander. Combine garlic, tomatoes, breadcrumbs, artichokes, cream, celery, salt, and cayenne in a saucepan, mixing well. Bring to a boil; cover and simmer 15 minutes, stirring occasionally. Sauté crabmeat and mushrooms in butter 5 minutes or until tender. Add crabmeat, mushrooms, green onions, parsley, ham, and sherry to artichoke mixture; stir well. Simmer 5 minutes, stirring occasionally. Remove from heat; cover and chill 1 to 2 hours. Place one oyster in each shell. Moisten each with about 1 teaspoon reserved liquid, and spoon chilled mixture evenly over top. Place filled shells on a bed of rock salt on a baking sheet, and bake at 450° for 8 minutes. Sprinkle each oyster with about 1 teaspoon Parmesan cheese, and bake an additional 5 minutes or until cheese melts and browns slightly. Serve with lemon wedges.

Yield: 6 to 8 servings
Joseph Broussard

Scallops Yvonne

16 ounces fresh
  scallops, blanched
1 quart heavy cream
4 ounces butter
4 ounces all-purpose
  flour
2 tablespoons chopped

fresh basil
1 tablespoon seasoning
  salt
2 shots Tabasco
16 toasted French
  bread rounds

Blanch scallops in 1 cup water until white or opaque in color. Drain scallops, and set aside; reserve liquid. Combine liquid with heavy cream in a saucepan, and bring to a boil. Meanwhile heat butter, and add flour; whisk rapidly, being cautious not to brown. Remove from heat, and add to boiling cream mixture, stirring until the cream coats the back of the spoon. Add fresh basil, seasoning salt, and Tabasco. Drop scallops in cream mixture, and reheat. Place 2 to 3 scallops on top of toasted French bread. Ladle sauce over scallops.

Yield: 8 servings
Bill Bell

You can serve this as an appetizer garnished with fresh basil leaves.

In 1989, Bill had just begun dating a girl named Yvonne, so he named the recipe for her. The recipe was a winner, as was the girl — she's now his wife.

Use Milnot evaporated milk and thicken with cornstarch instead of butter and flour.

secretsecretsecretsecretsecretsecretsecretsecretsecretsecretsecretsecret

You need to use Langlinais French bread, if possible. It's made in Lafayette. Tabasco gives the dish that needed punch.

Smoked Shrimp Cheesecake

¹/₂ **pound shrimp (70 to 90 count), peeled**
Breadcrumbs
Butter
1¹/₂ pounds cream cheese
5 whole eggs
¹/₃ cup flour

¹/₄ **cup Thousand Island dressing**
¹/₄ **cup smoked shrimp stock**
4 ounces red bell pepper, roasted and diced

Smoke shrimp in a smoker in a pan or on a BBQ pit in a pan for about 20 minutes. Let cool, and reserve smoked shrimp stock. Place breadcrumbs and butter in the bottom of a springform pan to form the crust, about ¹/₈ to ¹/₄ inch thick. In a mixer, place softened cream cheese, eggs, flour, Thousand Island dressing, and smoked shrimp stock; mix on low until smooth. Chop shrimp and roasted peppers, and mix. Pour half of cream cheese mixture into pan, add shrimp and peppers, and top with the rest of the cream cheese mixture. Bake at 300° for 40 minutes or until top of cheese cake is golden brown. Let cool for 3 hours at room temperature then refrigerate overnight.

Yield: 10 servings
Bill Bell

Serve chilled before dinner with a hearty bottle of Bordeaux or a Sauvignon Blanc.

Substitute light cream cheese or Neufchâtel cheese; use egg substitute instead of whole eggs.

secretsecretsecretsecretsecretsecretsecretsecretsecretsecretsecretsecret
The fresh shrimp stock makes this dish so flavorful, especially since it is smoked.

Trote Involtini

GOLD—1990

½ pound cleaned
  crawfish tails
½ pound jumbo lump
  crabmeat
¼ gallon oysters
¼ cup chopped green
  onions
½ cup white wine
1 cup Parmesan cheese
3 tablespoons crushed
  garlic, divided
Juice of 3 lemons,
  divided
1 tablespoon crushed
  oregano
1 cup breadcrumbs
1 cup béchamel cream
1 tablespoon salt
1 tablespoon pepper
10 (8-ounce) deboned
  rainbow trout
½ cup cracked black
  peppercorns
2 tablespoons olive oil
1 cup butter
1 tablespoon parsley
¼ cup water

Place crawfish, crabmeat, oysters, green onions, and wine in pot; bring to boil. Cook for 3 minutes; strain and cool. Once cooled, place in bowl with Parmesan cheese, 2 tablespoons garlic, juice of 2 lemons, oregano, breadcrumbs, béchamel cream, salt, and pepper. Mix well. Stuff cavity of fish, and sew shut. Sprinkle peppercorns on fish. Heat olive oil in skillet until oil begins to smoke. Place fish in skillet, and cook 6 to 8 minutes on each side. Remove fish, and discard excess oil. Place butter, juice from 1 lemon, 1 tablespoon garlic, a pinch of salt and pepper, parsley, and water in same skillet. Let mixture reduce then pour over fish.

Yield: 10 servings
Brian J. Blanchard

secretsecretsecretsecretsecretsecretsecretsecretsecretsecretsecretsecret
Fry the fish in very hot olive oil in a well-ventilated area. It creates a crispy outside "crust" to contrast with the moist stuffing inside.

BRONZE—1993

Artichoke Acadian with Bienville Sauce

10 artichoke bottoms
2 teaspoons all-purpose
    seasoning, divided
3 ounces egg wash
5 ounces hazelnut flour
³/₄ cup butter, divided
3 ounces celery
3 ounces onion
3 ounces bell pepper

3 ounces parsley
2 ounces green onions
¹/₄ pound lump
    crabmeat
1 teaspoon lobster base
1 ounce Parmesan
    cheese
2 ounces cream cheese
1 cup breadcrumbs

Season artichokes with 1 teaspoon seasoning, and dip in egg wash and flour; then sauté in ¹/₄ cup butter. Let drain on paper napkin. Melt ¹/₂ cup butter, and sauté celery and next 4 ingredients. Add crabmeat, lobster base, and 1 teaspoon seasoning. Sauté, and then add Parmesan, cream cheese, and breadcrumbs; mix well. Stuff artichokes. Serve with Bienville Sauce.

Bienville Sauce:
¹/₂ cup butter
2 teaspoons chopped
    onion
4 teaspoons flour
¹/₂ cup white wine
¹/₄ pound shrimp (90 to
    110 count)

1 teaspoon chicken
    base
¹/₄ cup chopped
    mushrooms
Red and black pepper
    to taste
¹/₂ cup cream

Melt butter, and sauté onion. Add flour, wine, shrimp, chicken base, and mushrooms. Add seasoning and cream. Let cook for 15 minutes. Run through fine strainer.

Yield: 10 servings
Patrick Breaux

secretsecretsecretsecretsecretsecretsecretsecretsecretsecretsecretsecret

Professional bases are a key ingredient in restaurant dishes, such as chicken base in this recipe.

Snapper Barrataria

4 (6-ounce) fillets of
   Talapia or similar fish
All-purpose seasoning
   to taste
1/2 cup butter, divided
1 cup sliced
   mushrooms
1/2 cup cherry tomatoes,
   halved

Dash of Worcestershire
   sauce
3 ounces white wine
1/2 cup green onions
1/2 pound lump
   crabmeat or crawfish
   tails

Season all fillets. Heat a heavy iron skillet. Add half the butter. Brown fish on both sides. Take fillets from pan; set aside. Add rest of butter to skillet, and sauté mushrooms and tomatoes. Add Worcestershire sauce, and let simmer. Add a little seasoning to taste. Stir in white wine, green onions, and crabmeat. Put fish in pan in a 350° oven until done. To serve, put fish on plate, and top with sauce.

Yield: 4 servings
Patrick Breaux

Stuffed Flounder En Croute

SILVER—1989

1/2 cup (total) chopped
   onion, bell pepper,
   and celery
1 1/2 ounces butter
1 ounce crawfish
1 ounce crabmeat (claw
   or lump)
2 ounces shrimp
2 ounces smoked
   oysters
Pinch of seasonings

Pinch of parsley
1 teaspoon green
   onions
2 eggs
1 cup of breadcrumbs
Pinch of Parmesan
   cheese
10 ounces fillet of
   flounder
1 sheet of puff pastry
1 egg

Sauté onion, pepper, and celery in butter. Add all of seafood; cook until done. Add seasonings, parsley, and green onions; simmer 10 minutes. Remove from heat, and add eggs, breadcrumbs, and Parmesan. Stuff flounder with seafood mixture. Wrap puff pastry around flounder, and brush with egg. Cook in 350° oven until pastry is brown. Slice and serve.

Yield: 10 servings
Patrick Breaux

BRONZE—1991

Roulades of Salmon with Crawfish

1 stalk celery, chopped	1 egg
1 onion, chopped	1 cup breadcrumbs
1 bell pepper, chopped	1 leek, lightly steamed
1 pound crawfish tails	2 pounds salmon fillets
3 ounces butter	1 package phyllo dough
1 teaspoon mixed seasoning, divided	Lemon Creole Sauce

Sauté celery, onion, bell pepper, and crawfish in butter in a small skillet. Remove from skillet, and add half a teaspoon of mixed seasoning, egg, and breadcrumbs. Wrap leek around stuffing. Pound salmon fillets lightly. Wrap salmon around stuffing; then wrap the whole product with 4 sheets of phyllo dough. Cook at 350° oven until brown. Slice and serve over Lemon Creole Sauce.

Lemon Creole Sauce:

4 ounces dark roux	1 small can tomato paste
1 onion, chopped	
1 bell pepper, chopped	3 pints shrimp or seafood stock
3 stalks celery, chopped	1 lemon
1 tablespoon mixed seasoning	

Make dark roux of flour and butter. Add chopped vegetables and seasoning. Sauté; then add tomato paste. Once paste is brown, add seafood stock and juice and rind of lemon. Cook over low heat for 1 hour. Strain.

Yields: 10 servings
Patrick Breaux

secretsecretsecretsecretsecretsecretsecretsecretsecretsecretsecretsecret
The crispy phyllo gives good contrast to the soft filling.

Seafood Eggplant Dressing

1 onion, chopped
1/2 stalk celery, chopped
1 bell pepper, chopped
1 cup butter
2 eggplants, peeled and chopped
1 pound lump crabmeat
1 (16-ounce) jar of oysters
1 pound shrimp (50 to 60 count)
3 ounces pimiento
1/2 bunch onion tops, chopped
2 teaspoons salt
2 tablespoons red pepper
1 teaspoon white pepper
2 eggs
1/2 cup chopped parsley
Breadcrumbs (about 3/4 cup)

Sauté onion, celery, and bell pepper in butter until cooked. Add eggplant, and let cook for 20 minutes. Add crabmeat, oysters, shrimp, pimiento, onion tops, and all seasonings. Let cook for 15 minutes on medium heat. Add eggs, parsley, and enough breadcrumbs for desired thickness. Place in greased casserole dish, and bake at 350° for 20 to 30 minutes.

Yield: 4 to 6 servings
Michael Chaisson C.W.C.

Shrimp Creole

1 onion, chopped
1 bell pepper, chopped
4 single stalks of celery, finely chopped
Vegetable oil
1 (12-ounce) can tomato paste
1 quart shrimp stock
1 tablespoon chicken base
1 tablespoon thyme
1 tablespoon sugar
1 tablespoon Lea & Perrins Worcestershire sauce
Tony Chachere's Creole Seasoning to taste
1 bunch onion tops, chopped
2 pounds shrimp (31 to 35 count)
Blond roux
Hot cooked rice

Sauté onion, bell pepper, and celery in skillet with oil until vegetables are limp or transparent. Add tomato paste and shrimp stock; let cook for 1/2 hour over medium heat. Add chicken base, thyme, sugar, Worcestershire sauce, seasoning, and onion tops. Let cook for another 15 minutes. Add shrimp and roux; let simmer for 5 minutes. Serve over rice.

Yield: 4 servings
Michael Chaisson C.W.C.

secretsecretsecretsecretsecretsecretsecretsecretsecretsecretsecretsecret
This dish definitely needs Tony Chachere's Creole Seasoning.

Snapper Royale

4 (8-ounce) snapper
  fillets
1 teaspoon salt
1 tablespoon red
  pepper
1 teaspoon paprika
1 onion, chopped
$\frac{1}{2}$ pound butter
2 pounds peeled shrimp
8 ounces mushroom
  stems and pieces

$\frac{1}{2}$ bunch onion tops,
  finely chopped
2 cups milk
1 tablespoon
  Worcestershire sauce
4 drops Louisiana Gold
  Pepper sauce
1 cup all-purpose flour
$\frac{1}{2}$ cup white wine

Bake snapper with salt, red pepper, and paprika in oven at 350° for $\frac{1}{2}$ hour or until brown. Sauté onion in butter. Add shrimp, and cook until pink. Stir in mushrooms, onion tops, milk and next 2 ingredients; let cook for 10 minutes. Add desired amount of flour, until the mixture thickens. Stir in wine.

Yield: 4 servings
Michael Chaisson C.W.C.

One snapper per person with 3 ounces sauce on top fish.

secretsecretsecretsecretsecretsecretsecretsecretsecretsecretsecretsecret
Hooray for the Louisiana Gold Pepper sauce.

Spicy Shrimp Mold

Use low-fat or fat-free cream cheese and Thousand Island dressing.

2 tablespoons
  unflavored gelatin
2 tablespoons cold
  water
2 tablespoons
  Zatarain's Crab Boil
  Liquid Seasoning
$\frac{1}{4}$ cup boiling water
8 ounces cream cheese
8 ounces Thousand
  Island dressing

1 teaspoon horseradish
1 tablespoon lemon
  juice
$\frac{1}{2}$ teaspoon salt
$2\frac{1}{2}$ cups cooked
  shrimp, chopped
$\frac{1}{2}$ cup chopped celery
$\frac{1}{4}$ cup chopped green
  bell pepper

Soften gelatin in cold water; add crab boil liquid seasoning. Add boiling water, and stir until dissolved. Add remaining ingredients, and pour into a mold. Refrigerate until congealed.

Yield: 8 servings
Lynn Epstein, LDN, RD

Prepare 1 day ahead to let seasonings mix. Try individual molds and serve on a bed of romaine lettuce and tomato wedges.

Cajun Red Hot Jambalaya

1 cup chopped onions
1 cup chopped celery
4 cups chopped
  eggplant
1 (10-ounce) can diced
  tomatoes and green
  chiles
12 ounces tomato
  sauce
¼ cup oil
⅔ pound hot smoked
  sausage links, sliced
3 cups long-grain rice,
  uncooked

3 bay leaves
1 tablespoon cayenne
  pepper
2 pounds tiny shrimp
4 cups chicken broth
1 tablespoon salt
2 tablespoons chow
  chow
¼ cup chopped green
  onions
2 tablespoons chopped
  parsley

Sauté onion, celery, eggplant, tomatoes, and tomato sauce in oil for 30 minutes. Add sausage and next 7 ingredients; cook on medium high heat until rice absorbs stock. Cover and reduce heat. Cook for 25 minutes. Add green onions and parsley; let stand for 10 minutes.

Yield: 4 to 6 servings
William Menard

secretsecretsecretsecretsecretsecretsecretsecretsecretsecretsecretsecret

Eggplant tones down the tomatoes and adds a smooth texture to this dish. Cajuns use chow chow to enhance soups, jambalayas, and gumbos.

GOLD—1993

Charred Tuna Laredo

1 ½ pounds fresh tuna
Salt and pepper
Olive oil
Pilaf

Crêpes
Tequila Salsa Beurre
Blanc

Cut tuna into 1-inch strips. Season tuna, and sear in olive oil in hot skillet until medium rare. To serve, place Pilaf on plate. Add tuna wrapped in crêpe. Top with Tequila Salsa Beurre Blanc.

Pilaf:

½ onion, chopped
½ red bell pepper,
  chopped
1 poblano, chopped
½ cup cooked corn
1 tomato, deseeded
  and diced

¼ cup black beans
Olive oil
2 cups cooked rice
Cilantro
Salt and pepper to taste
1 avocado, chopped
1 mango, chopped

Sauté onion, peppers, corn, tomato, and beans in olive oil. Add rice, cilantro, and salt and pepper. Remove from heat, and add avocado and mango. Keep warm.

Crêpes:

2 eggs
1 cup milk
2 ounces all-purpose
  flour
2 ounces mesa flour
1 tablespoon butter,
  melted

1 tablespoon sugar
Salt to taste
Cumin to taste
¼ cup pureed cooked
  corn
2 ounces pureed cooked
  black beans

In mixing bowl, whip eggs, and add milk. Add flours, and work by hand until mixed. Add butter, sugar, and seasonings. Divide mixture in half, and add corn puree to half and black bean puree to the other. Pour each mixture into half of skillet, and cook. Set aside.

Tequila Salsa Beurre Blanc:

1 cup Tequila
1 cup white wine
Juice of 1 lemon
Juice of 1 lime
2 teaspoons coconut
  milk
3 tomatoes, deseeded
  and chopped
1 purple onion, diced
1 roasted poblano
  pepper, chopped

1 roasted anaheim
  pepper, chopped
1 jalapeño, chopped
1 teaspoon fresh
  cilantro, chopped
½ sweet red pepper,
  chopped
½ teaspoon cumin
1 pound unsalted
  butter, cut in pieces

(Continued on next page)

Charred Tuna Laredo (continued)

Mix first 13 ingredients in saucepan; simmer. Reduce until almost all liquid has evaporated. Add cold butter a little at a time. Keep salsa warm.

Yield: 10 servings
Eric Fincke

secretsecretsecretsecretsecretsecretsecretsecretsecretsecretsecretsecretsecret
The combination of the crêpe and the sweetness of the salsa makes this dish special.

Crab Cakes with Creole Sauce

¼ **cup horseradish**
¼ **cup fresh lemon juice**
2 tablespoons minced green onions
2 tablespoons minced celery
2 tablespoons minced green bell pepper
2 garlic cloves, minced
1 tablespoon minced parsley
Salt to taste
Pepper to taste
Tabasco to taste

½ **cup olive oil**
1 egg
3 tablespoons whipping cream
1 teaspoon dry mustard
1 tablespoon chopped parsley
Salt to taste
Pepper to taste
Tabasco to taste
1 pound crabmeat
1½ tablespoons all-purpose flour
¼ **cup butter**

Bake the crab cakes instead of sautéing them.

Mix first 10 ingredients in a bowl. Whisk in olive oil slowly. Taste for seasoning. This should be made 1 day in advance and refrigerated. Beat egg and next 6 ingredients for crab cakes in a bowl. Mix crabmeat and flour then combine with egg mixture. Form into 12 round cakes. Heat butter in skillet until hot. Add crab cakes, and cook until brown on both sides. Drain on paper towels. Serve with horseradish sauce on the side.

Yield: 6 servings
Joe Gonsoulin

Arrange on plates, and garnish with lemon wedges and parsley. Serve sauce separately.

secretsecretsecretsecretsecretsecretsecretsecretsecretsecretsecretsecretsecret
Fresh Gulf crabmeat is the key to this dish.

GOLD—1993

This is an elegant dish with a great degree of simplicity. The flavors are explosive and the rewards have been golden.

Swordfish Swan Lake

3 pounds swordfish, cut into 12-inch-long cylinders
8 cups water
2 cups pineapple juice
4 large hickory-smoked sweet potatoes
1 large hickory-smoked Idaho potato
½ teaspoon cinnamon
2 tablespoons brown sugar
Pinch of nutmeg
1 parsnip
1 carrot
1 beet
Lobster Madeira Sauce

Marinate swordfish for 12 hours in water and pineapple juice. Remove from marinade and drain: set aside. Smoke sweet potatoes and Idaho potato. Remove skin, placing pulp in a mixing bowl. Add cinnamon, brown sugar and nutmeg to mixing bowl, and process until smooth. Place in a pastry bag with a star tip, and set aside. Peel parsnip, carrot, and beet; cut julienne style. Steam al dente, and set aside. Charbroil swordfish cylinders. Cut swordfish at a 45° angle in 1-, 2- and 3-inch pieces, to equal 3.5 ounces of swordfish (cooked weight). In the center of the plate, pipe sweet potatoes into a circle measuring 4 inches in circumference and ¾ inches in height. Place plate under broiler for 2 minutes until the edges of the sweet potatoes are browned. Ladle 2 ounces of Lobster Madeira Sauce in center of potatoes, and stand the swordfish upright in the sauce. Fan vegetables to the outside of the smoked potatoes in 3 points, creating a triangle effect around the sweet potatoes on the plate. Garnish with 3 sautéed parsnip daisies.

Lobster Madeira Sauce:
2 tablespoons olive oil
6 (1-pound) Maine lobsters
½ cup diced Vidalia onions
¼ cup diced carrots
¼ cup Madeira wine
8 cups water
1 teaspoon Tabasco sauce
¼ cup butter
1 teaspoon chopped fresh garlic
3 tablespoons cornstarch
¼ cup water

In an 8-quart saucepan, heat 2 tablespoons olive oil over medium high. Cut lobsters into half lengthwise, and remove meat (freeze meat for another use). Sauté lobster shells in hot olive oil, browning all sides. Add onions and carrots, and sauté 5 minutes. Deglaze pan with ¼ cup Madeira wine. Add 8 cups water and Tabasco sauce. In a small saucepan over high heat, brown ¼ cup butter until brown specks appear in the bottom. Carefully skim all clarified butter from the pan and discard, reserving only the brown specks in the bottom. Add the brown specks to

(Continued on next page)

Swordfish Swan Lake (continued)

the stock. Add garlic. Boil for 30 minutes, reducing by half. Strain stock through cheesecloth into new saucepan. Bring to a boil, and thicken with the cornstarch and water mixture.

Yield: 10 servings
James Graham

Fried Smoked Rock Shrimp and Corn Beignets

1 ½ cups all-purpose flour	12 cloves garlic, roasted and minced
2 eggs	2 tablespoons cilantro, chopped
1 cup beer	1-2 jalapeños, chopped
1 teaspoon salt	½ purple onion, minced
1 tablespoon baking powder	1 teaspoon cumin powder
1 pound rock shrimp	1 pound angel hair pasta, cooked
1 cup cooked corn	2 quarts vegetable oil
1 roasted red bell pepper, diced	

Mix first 5 ingredients until blended; then add next 8 ingredients, and blend well. Take a heaping tablespoon of batter, and wrap pasta around it; lightly press into roll. Heat oil to 325°, and drop beignets into oil; fry approximately 5 minutes. Top with Alfredo, Pesto or Marinara Sauce.

Yield: 8 to 10 servings
Eric Fincke

Fried Catfish

1 tablespoon salt	4 (8-ounce) catfish fillets
1 teaspoon garlic powder	2 eggs
1 teaspoon ground white pepper	3 cups milk
½ teaspoon ground red pepper	4 cups all-purpose flour
	4 cups breadcrumbs
	4 cups peanut oil

Combine first 4 ingredients in a small bowl; mix well, and sprinkle over both sides of fish. Beat together eggs and milk. Dredge fillets through flour; dip in egg mixture, and then dredge through breadcrumbs. Heat peanut oil in heavy pot over high heat until very hot. Add fillets, and cook 5 minutes on each side or until browned.

Yield: 4 servings
Henry Gillett

This recipe was one of the early examples of the change to come to the art of Cajun cooking — the fusion of Creole and Cajun.

Redfish Louisiana

2 tablespoons oil
2 eggs
½ cup milk
½ cup buttermilk
3 cups all-purpose flour
Seasoning salt to taste
8 (10-ounce) redfish or other meaty fish fillets
3 tablespoons clarified butter
½ rib celery, chopped
¼ bell pepper, chopped
¼ small onion, chopped
1 clove garlic, minced
2 shallots, minced
1 pound crawfish tails
1 tablespoon crawfish fat
2 tablespoons all-purpose flour
½ cup shrimp stock
¼ cup white wine
Salt to taste
Pepper to taste
Trappey's hot sauce
1 tablespoon chopped parsley
¼ cup chopped green onions

Heat oil at 350°. Whip eggs and milks together. Season flour with seasoning salt. Dip fillets in egg batter, and dredge in flour. Drop fillets in hot oil; fry until golden brown. Heat 3 tablespoons clarified butter in sauté pan. Add celery, bell pepper, onion, garlic, and shallots. Sauté 2 minutes. Add crawfish tails, and sauté for 1 minute. Add crawfish fat and flour; cook an additional minute. Add shrimp stock and wine. Season to taste with salt, pepper, and hot sauce; cook another minute. Add parsley and green onions, and pour over redfish.

Yield: 8 to 10 servings
Patrick Mould C.E.C.

Alligator Bayou Courtableu

2 (6-ounce) alligator
  fillets
3 ounces tasso, sliced
  thinly
2 ounces Monterey Jack
  cheese, shredded
2 ounces mild Cheddar,
  shredded
3 ounces shrimp (50 to
  60 count), poached

¼ teaspoon salt
¼ teaspoon sugar
⅛ teaspoon red pepper
⅛ teaspoon black
  pepper
⅛ teaspoon garlic
  powder
1 egg
1 tablespoon milk
Flour (all-purpose)

Pound alligator fillets to ¼ inch thick without tearing. Lay out fillets, and spread with tasso, Monterey Jack cheese, Cheddar, and shrimp, leaving a ¾-inch border around the edge. Mix salt and next 4 ingredients; add to fillets. Preheat oven to 400°. Beat egg and milk together, and pour onto the ¾-inch border. Sprinkle with flour, and roll tightly, jelly roll style. Secure ends with toothpicks. Place rolls onto a generously greased casserole dish. Baste rolls with oil, margarine, or butter. Bake 20 minutes. Remove from oven. Cool on counter for 5 minutes before slicing. Remove toothpicks. Slice in ¾-inch-thick medallions. Pour Garlic Red Pepper Sauce onto bottom of serving platter. Arrange medallions on platter either side by side or slightly overlapped.

Garlic Red Pepper Sauce:
8 ounces clam juice
½ teaspoon red pepper
¼ cup finely diced
  onion
1 teaspoon minced
  fresh garlic

1 tablespoon blond
  roux
2 tablespoons butter
¼ cup heavy cream

In a small saucepan, add clam juice, red pepper, onion and garlic; bring to a boil. Add roux, stirring constantly for 1 minute. Remove from heat. Fold in butter and heavy cream until combined.

Yield: 4 servings
James Graham

This dish landed James the title of Le Chef de Cocodrie from LSU's Louisiana Agricultural Extension Service. It was a smash hit at a party for Julia Child and Robert Mondovi and the Bacchus Society and got rave reviews at a luncheon in D.C. for Sen. Breaux.

This dish is a tribute to "Big Al," the 14-foot-long stuffed alligator found in the center of Prejean's Restaurant. He's the largest alligator ever caught in South Louisiana.

Alligator Grand Chenier

4 alligator fillets
Salt
Red pepper
1/4 cup margarine
1/2 cup diced onion
1/4 cup diced bell pepper
1/4 cup diced celery
1 teaspoon salt
1/2 teaspoon red pepper
1/4 teaspoon black
   pepper

1/2 teaspoon garlic
   powder
2 chicken bouillon
   cubes
1 cup water
2 teaspoon chopped
   parsley
1 1/2 cups breadcrumbs
1/4 cup chopped
   scallions
1 egg
1 pound dark crabmeat

Carefully pound alligator into hand-size rectangles, without tearing meat. Lightly season with salt and red pepper to taste; set aside. In a large skillet, melt margarine, and sauté onion, pepper, and celery until tender. Add salt, peppers, and garlic powder, and stir. Dissolve bouillon cubes in water; add to mixture, and boil for 3 minutes. Remove from heat. Stir in remaining ingredients, carefully folding in the crabmeat last. Spoon stuffing onto alligator fillets; fold over "omelette style." Secure edges with wooden picks if desired. Grill in preheated 350° lightly greased skillet. Serve plain or with your favorite seafood sauce.

Yield: 8 servings
James Graham

Lump Crabmeat Fettuccini

1 pound fettuccini
  noodles
1 tablespoon olive oil
1 pint heavy whipping
  cream
1 tablespoon fresh basil
1 tablespoon chopped
  garlic
1 tablespoon chopped
  parsley

2 tablespoons chopped
  green onions
1 tablespoon seasoned
  salt
2 to 3 ounces grated
  Parmesan cheese,
  divided
½ pound lump
  crabmeat
8 crab claws

Cook noodles in boiling water with olive oil; set aside to cool. In large sauté pan, combine cream and next 5 ingredients. Add half the cheese, and reduce sauce. Add more cheese to thicken or more cream to loosen. Fold in crabmeat and crab claws, being careful not to break up crab. Warm mixture; do not overcook. Serve over fettuccini noodles.

Yield: 4 servings
Patrick Mould C.E.C.

Shrimp Mold

1½ pounds cooked
  shrimp, coarsely
  chopped
1 (10¾-ounce) can
  cream of shrimp soup,
  undiluted
1 cup shrimp or chicken
  broth
1 cup chopped green
  onions

1 cup finely chopped
  celery
1 (8-ounce) package
  cream cheese
½ cup mayonnaise
Dash of garlic powder
Creole seasoning to
  taste
3 (¼-ounce) envelopes
  plain gelatin

Use light cream cheese and light mayonnaise.

In a medium saucepan combine all ingredients except gelatin. Heat until cream cheese is melted, stirring constantly. Dissolve gelatin in small amount of water. Add to mixture, and heat until it bubbles. Pour into 6-cup mold, and chill at least 3 hours. Unmold on plate or platter.

Yield: 20 servings
William M. O'Dea C.E.C., A.A.C.

Garnish center of shrimp mold with kale, and surround mold with crackers of your choice.

Cajun Stuffed Shrimp

3 pounds shrimp
1 cup olive oil
5 tablespoons lemon
  juice
Tony Chachere's Creole
  Seasoning
2 tablespoons chopped
  parsley
½ cup olive oil
½ cup soft margarine
1 cup French
  breadcrumbs, toasted

¼ cup grated
  mozzarella cheese
½ cup grated Parmesan
  cheese
½ cup chopped green
  onions
½ cup chopped parsley
½ cup finely chopped
  tasso
½ teaspoon garlic
  powder
Parsley and lemon twist
  for garnish

Peel shrimp, butterfly, leave on tails. Mix marinade of 1 cup olive oil, lemon juice, Creole seasoning, and 2 tablespoons parsley. Marinade shrimp 1 hour at room temperature (or up to 24 hours in refrigerator). Remove shrimp from marinade. Mix ½ cup olive oil and next 8 ingredients; stuff shrimp. Place on broiler pan, and broil until browned about 4 minutes. Garnish with parsley and lemon twist.

Yield: 8 servings
William M. O'Dea C.E.C., A.A.C.

Shrimp may also be baked in the oven at 400°. The recipe can be made a day ahead of time and held in refrigerator.

This needs tasso and Tony Chachere's Seasoning to make it Cajun.

Cajun Grilled Shrimp

2 pounds shrimp,
  peeled and deveined
4 cups peanut oil
1 cup diced yellow
  onion
1 tablespoon chopped
  garlic

2 tablespoons Tony
  Chachere's Creole
  Seasoning
2 teaspoons cumin
1 teaspoon rosemary
1 teaspoon thyme

Marinate shrimp in peanut oil and remaining ingredients at room temperature for 1 hour or longer. Spear on skewers. Grill over hot coals 5 to 7 minutes, basting frequently with marinade. Serve hot with Cajun Butter.

Cajun Butter:

1 pound unsalted
  butter
2 teaspoons basil
2 teaspoons tarragon

2 teaspoons Tony
  Chachere's Creole
  Seasoning
1 teaspoon garlic
  powder
3 drops Tabasco sauce

Mix all ingredients well. Serve butter hot.

Yield: 4 servings

William M. O'Dea C.E.C., A.A.C.

These shrimp may also be grilled on flat grill.

SILVER—1991

Lonnie first tested this recipe at the Old Ice House restaurant, and the customers just loved it.

Soft Shell Excellence

10 soft shell crabs
  (gills and eyes
  removed)
3 teaspoons all-purpose
  seasoning, divided
2 eggs
1½ cups milk
3 medium onions, finely
  diced
4 ounces clarified
  butter
½ cup dry white wine
1 pound lump crabmeat
2 cups heavy whipping
  cream
¼ cup thinly sliced
  green onions
¼ cup finely chopped
  parsley
3 cups all-purpose flour
Peanut oil

Season crabs with 2 teaspoons all-purpose seasoning, and set aside. Make egg wash of eggs and milk; set aside. Sauté onion and butter together until onions are dark brown, but not burned. Deglaze pan with wine, and add remainder of seasoning. Add lump crabmeat, and sauté 2 to 3 minutes. Add cream, green onions, and parsley. While sauce is reducing, batter crabs in flour, then in egg wash, then flour again. Fry in peanut oil at 350° until golden brown. Top with lump crabmeat sauce, and garnish, if desired.

Yields: 10 servings
Lonnie Pope, Jr.

Serve as an entrée with garlic toast and steamed vegetables.

secretsecretsecretsecretsecretsecretsecretsecretsecretsecretsecretsecret

The sweetness of the sauce is achieved in the caramelization of the onions. Slow sautéing in this step will make a foolproof sauce.

BBQ Catfish New Orleans Style

6 catfish fillets	2 tablespoons Lea &
2 teaspoons all-purpose	Perrins
seasoning	Worcestershire sauce
2 medium onions,	1 (16-ounce) can beer
julienned	1 cup white wine
12 large mushrooms,	2 teaspoons cornstarch
sliced	1/4 cup water
1/2 cup butter	1/4 cup green onions
3 tablespoons Cajun	1/4 cup parsley
Power garlic sauce	

Season catfish with all-purpose seasoning, and bake at 350° for 25 to 30 minutes or until fish flakes when touched. Meanwhile, in a medium saucepan, begin sautéing onions, mushrooms, and butter. When onions are limp, add Cajun Power, Lea & Perrins, beer, and wine; bring to a boil. Reduce sauce for 5 minutes. Mix cornstarch and water; add to pot. Simmer for 5 minutes more. When fish is cooked, place one fillet on a plate, and top with sauce. Garnish with green onions and parsley.

Yield: 6 servings
Lonnie B. Pope, Jr.

Serve over hot rice or with garlic bread.

secretsecretsecretsecretsecretsecretsecretsecr
The Cajun Power garlic sauce gives this dish its terrific taste.

For years the chefs of New Orleans have barbecued shrimp. Lonnie decided to vary their sauce recipe and try another seafood. A customer who was allergic to shrimp was thrilled with his decision.

Replace the butter with water, and use a light beer. This reduces the fat content of the recipe by about three-fourths.

Stuffed Red Snapper with Shrimp and Crabmeat Cream Sauce

1 ½ pounds red snapper fillets
1 tablespoon salt
1 tablespoon onion powder
1 tablespoon garlic powder
1 tablespoon white pepper
1 tablespoon oregano
1 tablespoon sweet basil
2 teaspoons red pepper
3 tablespoons butter
1 cup finely chopped onion
¼ cup finely chopped green bell pepper
¼ cup finely chopped red bell pepper
¼ cup finely chopped celery
5 ounces small shrimp, peeled
1 cup heavy cream
1 cup fine breadcrumbs
½ pound fresh lump crabmeat
Vegetable cooking spray
Cream Sauce

Cut each fillet in half lengthwise, being careful not to cut all the way through (this will form a pocket). Combine salt and next 6 seasonings in a small bowl; mix well, and sprinkle 1 ½ tablespoons over both sides of fish and inside cavity. Reserve remaining seasoning. For stuffing, melt the butter in a medium skillet over high heat. Add the onion, both bell peppers, celery, and 1 tablespoon of the seasoning mix. Cook and stir 5 minutes. Add the shrimp; cook 5 minutes, stirring constantly. Stir in the cream, and cook 5 minutes longer. Remove from heat, and carefully fold in the breadcrumbs and crabmeat; set aside, and let cool to touch. Place fillets on a clean flat surface. Spoon equal portions of stuffing mixture into cavity of each. Close cavities, and place fillets on a baking sheet that has been sprayed with vegetable cooking spray. Place in broiler about 7 inches from heat; broil 10 to 12 minutes or until fish flakes easily with a fork. Remove from heat. Place each fillet on a plate, and spoon equal portions of the Cream Sauce over each. Serve hot.

Cream Sauce:
3 tablespoons butter, divided
4 ounces small shrimp, peeled
1 cup fresh mushrooms, thinly sliced
¼ cup finely chopped green onions
2 teaspoons reserved seasoning mix
1 cup whipping cream

(Continued on next page)

Stuffed Red Snapper with Shrimp and Crabmeat Cream Sauce (continued)

In a medium skillet over high heat, melt 2 tablespoons of the butter. Add the shrimp, mushrooms, green onions, and seasoning. Cook and stir constantly. When shrimp begin to stick to skillet, add the cream; cook and stir 5 minutes. Add the remaining butter, and cook 3 to 4 minutes longer or until sauce thickens.

Yield: 4 servings
Enola Prudhomme

Enola's Catfish in Red Gravy

3 pounds fresh catfish fillets
1 teaspoon salt
1 teaspoon red pepper
1 teaspoon black pepper
¼ cup unsalted butter
1 cup finely chopped onion
1 cup finely chopped celery
1 cup finely chopped bell pepper
1 cup catsup
3 tablespoons all-purpose flour
½ cup water
½ cup finely chopped green onion tops

Cut fillets into ¾-inch-thick pieces. Sprinkle the salt, red pepper, and black pepper over both sides of fish; set aside. Melt the butter in a large heavy skillet over medium heat. Add the onion, celery, and bell pepper; cook and stir 5 minutes or until onions are transparent. Add the catsup; reduce the heat to simmer, and cook, covered, 15 to 18 minutes. Dissolve the flour in the water, and add to skillet, along with the fish. Add the onion tops, and cook 10 to 12 minutes longer, or until fish is tender, shaking skillet to prevent sticking.

Yield: 6 servings
Enola Prudhomme

Enola's Catfish Over Seafood

½ pound boneless
  catfish, chopped
½ pound small shrimp,
  peeled and deveined
2 cups water
1 teaspoon salt, divided
1 teaspoon ground red
  pepper, divided
4 tablespoons
  margarine
2 cups chopped onion
½ cup chopped bell
  pepper
½ pound claw crabmeat

1 cup fine dry
  breadcrumbs
1 teaspoon browning-
  and-seasoning sauce
1 tablespoon salt
1½ tablespoons ground
  red pepper
6 (8-ounce) catfish
  fillets
2 eggs
2 cups milk
2 cups all-purpose flour
1 cup vegetable oil,
  divided

In a 5-quart Dutch oven over high heat, add chopped catfish, shrimp, water, ½ teaspoon salt and ¼ teaspoon of red pepper. Bring to a boil, and boil 10 minutes. Remove from heat, and set aside. Melt the margarine in a medium skillet over medium heat. Add onion, bell pepper, and the remaining salt and red pepper; cook and stir 10 minutes, and then add to Dutch oven. Return Dutch oven to medium heat, and add the crabmeat, breadcrumbs, and browning sauce, stirring well. Cook and stir 3 minutes longer. Sprinkle salt and red pepper over fillets. Beat together eggs and milk. Dredge fillets through flour; dip in egg and milk mixture, then dredge again in flour. Heat ½ cup oil in a large skillet until very hot. Add 3 fillets, and cook 3 to 4 minutes on both sides. Repeat process until all fillets are cooked. Serve over seafood stuffing. Top with a light cheese, if desired.

Yield: 6 servings
Enola Prudhomme

Poisson Arme Braisee à la Moelle

BRONZE—1990

4 pounds swordfish
   fillet
6 ounces bacon,
   julienned
4 shallots, finely
   minced
6 large mushrooms,
   julienned
2 carrots, julienned
1½ finely minced
   onions
1½ cups dry Sémillon
1½ cups fond de veau
1 teaspoon salt

1 teaspoon white
   pepper
1 teaspoon cayenne
1 teaspoon chopped
   lemon thyme
1 teaspoon chopped
   dillweed
10 cloves garlic
30 jumbo shrimp,
   peeled, deveined, and
   tail left on
Sprigs of lemon thyme
   and dill
10 ounces blanched
   veal bone marrow

Place first 13 ingredients in a well-buttered gratin dish. Add garlic cloves and shrimp. Place in a 425° oven (conventional). Bake, continually basting the fish until it's glazed and golden brown. When the fish is cooked, serve on individual plates on a bed of the vegetables and sauce, and top each with a roasted garlic clove and sprigs of lemon thyme and dill. Garnish with the shrimp and the veal bone marrow.

Yield: 10 servings
Bryan Richard

SILVER — 1988

Zappa di Pesce (Italian Fish Soup)

This is already a light recipe.

½ pound amberjack fillet
½ pound ling, cobia, or lemonfish
½ pound wahoo or ono
½ pound black drum
½ pound swordfish
2 gallons fish stock
2 white onions, minced
3 sprigs fresh thyme
3 cups dry white wine

3 cups fresh tomatoes, peeled, seeded, and diced
¼ cup fresh garlic, chopped
2 tablespoons saffron threads
1 tablespoon cayenne
1 tablespoon white pepper
1 cup basil chiffonade
Cornstarch and water

Dice all fish in half-inch squares; set aside. Combine fish stock and next 8 ingredients; cook for 20 minutes. Add the fish and basil to the stock. Simmer 10 to 12 minutes; then thicken with cornstarch dissolved in water.

Yield: 6 servings
Bryan Richard

Fish stock enriched with shrimp stock makes for a tasty recipe. Introducing fish too early into the hot mixture may cause excessive disintegration.

secretsecretsecretsecretsecretsecretsecretsecretsecretsecretsecret

The soup, china, and silver have to be absolutely hot, and the steamy broth, all herbal and tasty, can be pushed to the limit.

Roulade de Poisson Rouge

GOLD — 1983

1 small white onion,
  minced
4 cloves garlic, minced
1 pound Louisiana
  crawfish tails
1 pound Louisiana
  shrimp
¼ cup sweet cream
  butter
1 red bell pepper,
  roasted, skinned, and
  minced
1 tablespoon basil
  chiffonade
1 cup dry vermouth,
  divided

1 teaspoon fresh thyme
1 teaspoon cayenne
1 teaspoon white
  pepper
3 eggs
2 cups fresh
  breadcrumbs
1 pound Louisiana lump
  crab
4 (16-ounce) redfish or
  meaty fish fillets, cut
  lengthwise
Salt and white pepper
  to taste
Saffron Cream Sauce

Sauté the onion, garlic, crawfish, and shrimp together in butter for 5 minutes. Add the red bell pepper and the basil. Add ½ cup vermouth. Transfer the seafood to a food processor to make the stuffing. Add thyme, cayenne, and white pepper. Process until pureed. Add 3 eggs to bind, and process 15 seconds. Add 2 cups fresh breadcrumbs. Transfer mixture to a bowl, and fold in crab. Fill fish fillets, seasoned with salt and white pepper, with the stuffing, and roll into small turbans. Place this in a baking dish dotted with butter and ½ cup dry vermouth. Bake until fish flakes gently in a 350° oven. Serve Saffron Cream Sauce over fish.

Saffron Cream Sauce:

1 cup heavy whipping
  cream
1 teaspoon saffron
  threads

Pinch of salt
Pinch of white pepper
½ cup sweet cream
  butter

Combine all ingredients in a saucepan. Reduce volume by half until it coats the back of a spoon. Take care, as reducing cream tends to boil over.

Yield: 8 servings
Bryan Richard

A nice accompaniment to this meal might be sautéed zucchini strips or two expensive mushrooms — chanterelles, shiitakes, or oyster mushrooms — sautéed in butter.

When Bryan finished preparing this dish at a small restaurant, he was ready to leave for the Culinary Classic, when Paul Prudhomme and a caravan of 22 judges showed up for lunch. He managed to feed them, drive 15 miles to the competition before the 4 p.m. deadline, and win a gold medal... pretty spectacular.

Eliminate the cream and butter; use extra virgin olive oil. However, it may not win a gold medal without the butter and cream.

Bronzed Tilapia with Crabmeat Atchafalaya

1 quart chicken stock
1 cup white wine
1 cup diced yellow
   onions
$^1/_2$ cup red bell peppers
$^1/_2$ cup golden bell
   peppers
$^1/_2$ cup green bell
   peppers
1 can Rotel tomatoes
1 tablespoon chopped
   garlic
$^1/_4$ teaspoon white
   pepper
1 teaspoon Tabasco
1 teaspoon green
   peppercorns in water

1 tablespoon chopped
   fresh basil
1 tablespoon chopped
   fresh oregano
2 tablespoons blond
   roux
1 pound jumbo lump
   crabmeat
2 tablespoons seasoned
   salt (Bruce's or Tony
   Chachere's)
$^1/_4$ cup olive oil
10 (7-ounce) tilapia or
   firm fish fillets
$^1/_4$ cup white wine

You could thicken the sauce with cornstarch and water instead of blond roux.

In heavy stockpot combine chicken stock, white wine, onions, and red, golden, and green bell peppers (that have been roasted, peeled, seeded, and diced). and simmer 20 minutes. Add tomatoes, garlic, white pepper, Tabasco, and green peppercorns. Simmer an additional 20 minutes. Add basil and oregano. Tighten with blond roux. Add crabmeat, and heat throughout with breaking up lump crabmeat. Season fillets with seasoned salt. Let marinate $^1/_2$ hour. In large skillet add enough olive oil to barely coat bottom. When oil is sufficiently hot, place fillets in pan, and bronze on both sides until done. Do not overcook. Deglaze pan with white wine. Remove fillets from pan, and place on serving plate. Add crabmeat sauce to skillet incorporating pan deglaze. Lace around fillets. Garnish and serve.

Yield: 10 servings
Michael A. Richard

Cook this dish in a black iron skillet, and let the skillet get fairly hot; then add the oil, and place the fish in. To make your own seasoned salt use salt, cayenne pepper, black pepper, granulated garlic, granulated onion, and white pepper. Serve on warm plate with side of angel hair pasta tossed in a garlic chive and shallot butter. Garnish with lemon wedge and fresh basil.

secretsecretsecretsecretsecretsecretsecretsecretsecretsecretsecretsecret
The black iron skillet is essential. The sauce gives the fish that little extra heat to liven the taste buds.

Orzo Pasta, Crabmeat, and Asparagus

2 pounds fresh
  asparagus
½ quart water
1 tablespoon seasoned
  salt
1 pound orzo pasta
1 pound lump crabmeat
1 cup diced onions

½ cup diced green bell
  peppers
½ cup diced red bell
  peppers
¼ cup diced celery
4 tablespoons Shallot
  and Chive Butter

Cook asparagus in salted water until crisp-tender. The color should be bright green. Cooking times vary according to size of asparagus. Watch closely. When done, remove from water, and drain. Serve immediately, otherwise cool under cold running water to stop cooking. Cook pasta according to package directions. Rinse and cool down immediately after. In large skillet, combine onions, green bell pepper, red bell peppers, and celery along with 4 tablespoons Shallot and Chive Butter. Sauté until onions are caramelized. Add lump crabmeat, pasta, and asparagus. Toss until coated and warmed throughout.

Shallot and Chive Butter:

1 pound butter,
  softened
½ teaspoon granulated
  garlic
1 teaspoon minced
  shallots
1 teaspoon Tabasco
½ teaspoon granulated
  onion

¼ teaspoon paprika
¼ teaspoon cayenne
  pepper
½ cup chopped chives
2 teaspoons fresh
  lemon juice
½ teaspoon seasoned
  salt

In mixer with paddle, beat butter on medium speed until smooth and light. Blend in remaining ingredients. Save 4 tablespoons for recipe. Roll remainder in parchment paper, or store in covered container in refrigerator; it can also be frozen.

Yield: 6 servings
Michael A. Richard

Serve on warm plate, sprinkling grated Parmesan cheese over the top, if desired.

Roulade of Speckled Trout

1 cup butter
9 egg yolks
1 tablespoon lemon
  juice
1 teaspoon garlic
1 can Rotel tomatoes
4 ounces heavy cream
2 dozen smoked
  oysters
8 ounces bacon,
  cooked and crumbled
6 (8-ounce) speckled
  trout or orange
  roughy fillets
6 slices bacon
1 cup butter
1 pound crabmeat

8 ounces shrimp (70 to
  90 count)
1 red bell pepper,
  chopped
½ bunch green onions,
  chopped
8 ounces heavy cream
4 ounces jalapeño
  cheese
1 tablespoon chopped
  garlic
Red pepper to taste
Black pepper to taste
Thyme to taste
Salt to taste
8 ounces soft
  breadcrumbs

Melt butter; set aside. Whip egg yolks over low heat, and add melted butter slowly. Whip vigorously. Add lemon juice, garlic, tomatoes, and cream. Fold in smoked oysters and bacon; set sauce aside. Place fillets flat. Partially cook bacon. Place bacon lengthways along fillets. Make stuffing by melting 1 cup butter, and sautéing crabmeat and remaining ingredients. Spread stuffing evenly over the top of bacon, taking one end and rolling up to make a jellyroll effect. Place toothpick through center to hold together. Grill over mesquite wood until cooked thoroughly. Top trout roulades with sauce.

Yield: 6 servings
Britt Shockley

Oysters Ailene

2 dozen oysters　　　　**Crab-Shrimp Stuffing**
Roasted Red Bell
Pepper Stuffing

Shuck oysters, reserving shells and liquid. Place raw oysters in shell. Prepare Roasted Red Bell Pepper Stuffing and Crab-Shrimp Stuffing. Cover half of each oyster with one stuffing and the other half with the other stuffing. Bake at 350° for 15 minutes.

Roasted Red Bell Pepper Stuffing:

10 red bell peppers	1 red pepper
3 tablespoons butter	1 black pepper
1 large onion, chopped	1 teaspoon chopped
1 teaspoon oyster	garlic
liquid	1 teaspoon all-purpose
1 pound tasso, chopped	seasoning
Breadcrumbs	Salt

Roast red bell peppers over mesquite logs. Seed and remove skin; chop fine, and set aside. Melt butter, and sauté onion. Mix in red bell pepper and oyster liquid. Fold in tasso meat and season to taste. Thicken with breadcrumbs, if needed; add seasonings.

Crab-Shrimp Stuffing:

3 tablespoons butter	1 pound crabmeat
1 large onion, chopped	Breadcrumbs
8 ounces mushrooms,	Red pepper to taste
chopped	Black pepper to taste
2 pounds shrimp	All-purpose seasoning
3 cups heavy cream	to taste
½ cup vermouth	Salt to taste
1 teaspoon oyster	
liquid	

Melt butter. Sauté onion and mushrooms until tender. Add shrimp, heavy cream, vermouth, and oyster liquid. Cook 15 minutes or until shrimp are done. Fold in crabmeat. Use breadcrumbs to thicken, if needed. Season to taste.

Yield: 10 servings
Britt Shockley

Britt spent childhood vacations at a family camp at Grand Isle, Louisiana. Sometimes he spent entire days shucking oysters he had gathered after diving off the camp's pier. He named this recipe after his grandmother, Ailene, who cooked all those oysters.

Seafood Pitivier

The recipe was invented for a television cooking program, Tabasco Kitchen.

1 (8-ounce) fish fillet
¼ cup butter
½ onion, diced
¼ bell pepper, diced
1 tablespoon flour
¼ cup shrimp stock
½ cup whipping cream
½ pound crawfish

Granulated garlic to
    taste
Red pepper to taste
Black pepper to taste
Salt to taste
Tabasco to taste
2 puff pastry sheets

Grill fish, and set aside to cool. Melt butter; add onion and bell pepper, and cook until tender. Add flour, and cook for 3 minutes. Stir in shrimp stock, whipping cream, crawfish, and seasonings; cook until thickened. Pour out on cookie sheet to cool. Place puff pastry sheets on floured surface. Cut fish into 3-inch round pieces, and cut pastry sheets into 4-inch rounds using biscuit cutter. After crawfish mousse has set, cut with 3-inch biscuit cutter. Place pastry round on table and grilled fish round on top of pastry. Place crawfish mousse on top of fish round, and cover with other pastry sheet. Brush edges with egg wash, and crimp with a fork. Trim edges, and bake at 450° until golden brown. Serve immediately so pastry won't collapse.

Yield: 2 servings
Britt Shockley

secretsecretsecretsecretsecretsecretsecretsecretsecretsecretsecretsecret
This is an entrée that has been adapted from a French dessert.

Grilled Grouper with Lump Crabmeat

10 (4-ounce) grouper
  fillets
Salt
Red pepper
3 cups heavy whipping
  cream
1 tablespoon chicken
  base
1/2 cup oil
1/2 cup flour
1 teaspoon basil
1 teaspoon dill

1 teaspoon tarragon
1 teaspoon thyme
1/2 cup white Zinfandel
  wine
1 teaspoon granulated
  garlic
1 teaspoon granulated
  onion
1/2 teaspoon salt
1/2 teaspoon red pepper
1/2 pound lump
  crabmeat

Season grouper with salt and red pepper on both sides; set aside. Bring whipping cream to a boil in large saucepan. Whisk in chicken base and roux made of oil and flour. Simmer 3 minutes. Add remaining ingredients, and cook on low heat for 10 minutes. Grill grouper. Place grouper on dinner plates, ladle sauce over top, and serve hot. Garnish with parsley and cayenne pepper, if desired.

Yield: 10 servings
Chris Sogga

Steamed Lobster Tail on Herb Cream Sauce

2 cups heavy cream
1 teaspoon chicken
  base
1 tablespoon blond
  roux
1/2 teaspoon fresh basil
1/2 teaspoon fresh
  tarragon
1/2 teaspoon fresh thyme

1/2 teaspoon fresh dill
1 teaspoon granulated
  garlic
1 teaspoon granulated
  onion
1/2 teaspoon red pepper
4 (10-ounce) South
  American lobsters
12 slices tomato

To make herb cream sauce, put cream in saucepan, and bring to a boil. Add chicken base and blond roux. Simmer for 2 minutes. Add remaining ingredients except lobsters and tomatoes; cook on low heat. Steam lobsters; then crack open, and separate meat from shell. Grill tomato slices. Place herb cream sauce on plate. Then place lobster on both sides of plate with tomatoes in the middle.

Yield: 4 servings
Chris Sogga

Grilled Speckled Trout with Sundried Tomatoes

1 green bell pepper	1 tablespoon granulated
1 red bell pepper	garlic
1 yellow bell pepper	1 tablespoon granulated
½ gallon veal stock	onion
1 tablespoon beef base	½ cup sundried
½ cup blond roux	tomatoes
1 tablespoon Lea &	1 cup butter
Perrins	10 (8-ounce) speckled
Worcestershire sauce	trout
1 tablespoon fresh	1 teaspoon seasoning
lemon juice	salt

Roast all bell peppers. Peel and cut into julienne strips; set aside. Pour veal stock in a gallon pot, and bring to a boil on high fire. Stir in beef base and blond roux. Simmer for 5 minutes. Add Lea & Perrins, lemon juice, granulated garlic, granulated onion, roasted peppers, and sundried tomatoes. Cook on low heat for a few minutes. Add butter, and reduce heat to a warm setting; remove peppers. Season fish with seasoning salt, and grill. Place fish on plate. Ladle sauce over fish. Garnish with pepper strips.

Yield: 10 servings
Chris Sogga

SILVER—1992

Lump Crabmeat Belaise in Mango Coulis

1 green plantain	½ teaspoon black
3 tablespoons olive oil	pepper
⅛ cup fresh avocado,	½ teaspoon minced
peeled and diced	garlic
1 tablespoon diced	½ cup jumbo lump
onion	crabmeat
3 tablespoons lime	⅛ cup mayonnaise
juice	⅛ tablespoon salt
1 tablespoon chopped	1 mango
fresh chives	¼ teaspoon salt
⅛ tablespoon chopped	¼ teaspoon sugar
fresh cilantro	Sour cream

Cut plantain on bias into 12 slices. Heat olive oil. Let plantain fry until crisp. Mix avocado and next 9 ingredients. Layer avocado mixture on plantain slices. For Mango Coulis, puree mango; add salt and sugar. Place Mango Coulis on plate, top with plantain, and garnish with sour cream.

Yields: 6 servings
Derrick Trotter

Grilled Salmon Jordan

1 teaspoon olive oil
3 scallops, minced
½ onion, chopped
½ yellow bell pepper, chopped
¼ cup minced parsley
3 ounces shrimp (91 to 110 count), minced
Salt and pepper to taste
¼ tablespoon breadcrumbs
¼ tablespoon Parmesan cheese
2 (6-ounce) salmon fillets
Salt and pepper
Oyster-Mushroom Red Pepper Sauce

Heat oil. Sauté scallops, onion, and bell pepper. When onions liquify, add parsley and shrimp with salt and pepper. Reduce liquid to one-third. Add breadcrumbs and Parmesan cheese; keep warm. Season salmon with salt and pepper; place on grill. Remove when scored. Add scallop dressing to center, and roll fillet. Place in oven at 350° for 10 minutes. Remove and slice into medallions. Place Oyster-Mushroom Red Pepper Sauce on plates; top with stuffed fillets.

Oyster-Mushroom Red Pepper Sauce:
1 red bell pepper
½ white onion, diced
2 tablespoons butter
½ tablespoon white pepper and salt
½ cup dry vermouth
5 oyster mushrooms, divided
1 cup heavy cream

Roast bell pepper at 350° until skin softens. Remove outer skin and seeds, dice pepper, and sauté in butter with diced onions. Add salt and pepper and vermouth. Add 2 mushrooms. Puree after reducing sauce to a third. Pass through fine sieve. Add cream and reduce by a third. Add 3 blanched mushrooms for garnish.

Yield: 2 servings
Derrick Trotter

Serve with glazed beets and turnips with oyster mushrooms and duchess potatoes.

Shrimp & Roasted Pecan Cornbread Dressing

1 pound ground beef	1 pound small to
2 onions, diced	medium shrimp,
1 red bell pepper, diced	shelled and deveined
2 bell peppers, diced	2 cups water
2 stalks celery, thinly	1 tablespoon sage
sliced	2 bunches green onions,
Salt to taste	sliced
Red pepper to taste	2 cups pecans, roasted
1 box Jiffy cornbread	and chopped
mix	1 bunch parsley,
	chopped

Brown ground beef with onion, bell peppers, celery, salt and red pepper, slowly. In meantime, bake the cornbread at 350° until it is cooked dry. Remove from oven, and cool as beef completes cooking. Drain off fat. Add shrimp to beef mixture, and sauté into mixture as they turn pink; add about 2 cups water, and then begin to incorporate cornbread, making sure to leave cornbread in rather chunky pieces. Now add sage, green onions, pecans, and parsley; reduce heat (consistency should be moist not wet or dry). Place in 350° oven for 10 minutes or until slight crust developed.

Yield: 6 servings
Derrick Trotter

Try molding this dressing in small custard cups; invert on plate for a different approach to cornbread dressing.

Tuna Vera Cruz

1 large tomato, diced	$\frac{1}{8}$ teaspoon ground
1 small red onion, diced	oregano
1 small yellow onion,	$\frac{1}{2}$ teaspoon salt
diced	2 tablespoons lemon
1 jalapeño pepper,	juice
finely diced	2 cups Meunière Sauce
3 tablespoons cilantro,	6 (4-ounce) tuna loin
finely diced	steaks
$\frac{1}{4}$ teaspoon garlic	
powder	

In a mixing bowl, thoroughly combine the first nine ingredients. Reserve in refrigerator. Chargrill the tuna medium, about 2 minutes on each side. Sauté tomato mixture and 1 $\frac{1}{2}$ cups of Meunière Sauce. Place the rest of sauce on plates. Place tuna on top of sauce, and top with tomato mixture. Garnish and serve.

Meunière Sauce:

$\frac{1}{2}$ cup demiglaze	2 shallots, coarsely
$\frac{1}{2}$ cup white wine	chopped
	2 cups butter

Combine first 3 ingredients. Reduce by half the volume. Remove from heat, and incorporate butter, sliced into $\frac{1}{2}$-inch slices. Whip in butter a few pieces at a time; strain and reserve.

Yield: 6 servings
Ernesto Zamora

GOLD—1988

Kahlúa Grilled Shrimp on Angel Hair Pasta

4 pounds peeled shrimp (10 to 15 count)	2 tablespoons chopped basil
2 cups Kahlúa	2 tablespoons chopped thyme
2 cups honey	2 tablespoons chopped cilantro
1½ cups salad oil	4 cups veal stock
2 bottles Tiger Sauce	Cornstarch to thicken
2 tablespoons seasoned salt	2 tablespoons Worcestershire sauce
2 tablespoons chopped garlic	3 tablespoons chopped red pepper
2 tablespoons chopped parsley	1 pound angel hair pasta, cooked
2 ounces hot pepper sauce	Fresh cilantro for garnish

Marinate shrimp in Kahlúa and next 10 ingredients for several hours. Grill shrimp over charcoal fire with mesquite and hickory wood. In a saucepan, simmer veal stock and reduce; thicken with cornstarch. Add Worcestershire and red pepper. Add cooked pasta to reduced veal stock. Serve shrimp over the angel hair pasta. Garnish with fresh cilantro.

Yield: 6 servings
Kenneth D. Veron

Bronzed Tuna with Peppers in Garlic Sauce

½ cup Cajun Power Garlic Sauce	½ each red, green, and gold peppers, julienned
½ cup olive oil	¼ onion, julienned
4 (6-ounce) tuna steaks	1 tablespoon butter
Seasoned salt	Dash of Tabasco jalapeño sauce

Mix marinade of garlic sauce and olive oil. Marinate tuna steaks for 5 minutes. Remove; set aside, and reserve marinade. Heat black iron skillet, season tuna, and bronze the tuna steaks until medium rare (do not blacken the fish). Pour reserved marinade in sauté pan, and quickly sauté peppers and onion until tender. Add butter to thicken sauce and Tabasco jalapeño sauce to taste. Serve sauce over bronzed tuna.

Yield: 4 servings
Kenneth D. Veron

Serve with lumpy mashed potatoes laced with crushed elephant garlic.

secretsecretsecretsecretsecretsecretsecretsecretsecretsecretsecretsecret
Cajun Power Garlic Sauce is a must.

Meats

GOLD—1993

This is difficult from start to finish but was designed with one thing in mind: bringing home a gold for Lafayette. The mission was a success in 3 competitions. It's a dish for a very special occasion - but worth trying the challenge.

Vermillion Venison Wellington

4 venison tenderloins	Béarnaise Sauce
½ cup soy sauce	2 Hungarian red
½ cup pineapple juice	peppers, julienned
3 cups water	2 tablespoons butter
Pâté	Phyllo sheets
Brown Butter Madeira	2 cups clarified butter
Sauce	1 egg, beaten

Rinse tenderloins. Using a sharp knife, peel off all silver skin. In a shallow dish, marinate tenderloins in a mixture of soy sauce, pineapple juice, and water for 24 hours. Remove from marinade; dry with a towel. Brush with oil, and charbroil on very hot flame until meat is rare to medium rare (about 3 to 5 minutes). Refrigerate tenderloins. Sauté Hungarian pepper strips in 2 tablespoons butter; set aside. Prepare pâté. When pâté is cold, begin preparing the Wellington. Place phyllo leaves under a damp cloth. Place one leaf at a time onto a dry work table. Lightly brush each leaf with clarified butter, layering the leaves until 5 layers thick. In 4 rows, ½ inch apart, place strips of red pepper from end to end of dough. Place a thin slice of pâté (2 inches wide) the length of the dough over the red peppers. Place a venison tenderloin on top of pâté, and roll tightly. Egg wash the edges to seal the seam. Place on baking pan, and bake at 350° for 12 minutes (medium rare to medium). Place Wellington on a cutting board, and let stand for 10 minutes before slicing. Serve over Brown Butter Madeira Sauce, and top with Béarnaise.

Pâté:

½ pound white veal	6 tablespoons Madeira
½ pound goose liver	wine
½ pound venison liver	Salt to taste
2 eggs	Red pepper to taste
¼ cup heavy cream	Black pepper to taste
½ cup morel	4 slices lean bacon
mushrooms, diced	1 bay leaf
2 tablespoons truffles,	
minced	

Grind veal, goose liver, and venison liver 3 times through medium grinder. Place ground meats into a medium bowl. Add 2 beaten eggs, heavy cream, morels, truffles, and Madeira wine. Then add salt, red pepper, and black pepper, and fold together until smooth. Pour mixture into a 3½x7-inch bread pan coated with cold butter. Top pâté with bacon and bay leaf. Place pan in a larger pan

(Continued on next page)

Vermillion Venison Wellington (continued)

that has 1 inch of water in the bottom. Cover pâté with aluminum foil, and bake for 1 hour at 325°. Remove foil, and continue baking for 35 minutes. Cool pâté at room temperature for 1 hour. Remove bacon and bay leaf, and refrigerate.

Brown Butter Madeira Sauce:

2 cups rich venison stock	1 teaspoon Tabasco
1 teaspoon chopped garlic	1/2 cup butter
	3 tablespoons flour
	1/3 cup Madeira wine

In a heavy saucepan, heat venison stock; add garlic and Tabasco, and bring to a boil. In a second heavy saucepan, boil the butter, whisking continuously until the butter browns and forms multiple brown (almost black) specks on the bottom. Add all but 3 tablespoons brown butter to the first pan of venison stock. Add 3 tablespoons flour to the reserved brown butter to make the roux. Cook over medium heat for 5 minutes, whisking continuously. Thicken the brown butter venison stock with the brown butter roux, and add 1/3 cup Madeira wine. Let sauce boil for 5 minutes. Keep warm until ready to use.

Béarnaise Sauce:

2 teaspoons tarragon leaves	1/2 teaspoon Worcestershire sauce
2 tablespoons red wine vinegar	1/8 teaspoon Tabasco
3 small egg yolks	1/2 teaspoon lemon juice
3/4 cups clarified butter	1/8 teaspoon salt
	Pinch of cayenne pepper

Boil tarragon leaves in red wine vinegar until 90% evaporated; set aside. In a 2-quart stainless steel bowl, whip egg yolks until beaten. Place bowl over double boiler, and cook yolks, whipping continuously until thickened to the consistency of pudding. Remove from heat; in a thin stream, pour clarified butter into the yolks, whisking continuously. After the butter has been added, whisk in Worcestershire sauce, Tabasco, lemon juice, salt, and cayenne pepper. Add 2 teaspoons tarragon leaf. Mix well. Keep sauce warm until ready to use.

Yield: 10 servings
James Graham

Due to the small circumference of the venison tenderloin, the traditional brioche dough is inadequate due to the shrinkage of the tenderloin. Phyllo has been substituted.

Ever since James can remember, his family's flowerbeds in Helena, Montana, were full of fresh herbs. The reward for having a big old bush of tarragon is this jewel of a rabbit recipe. Easy enough to prepare every Sunday, and fit for a king.

Domestic Rabbit with Tarragon Cream Sauce

2 domestic rabbits	3 tablespoons chopped
3 tablespoons corn oil	fresh tarragon
1 teaspoon salt	1/4 teaspoon fresh thyme
1 teaspoon cayenne	leaves
pepper	1 large carrot
3/4 teaspoon granulated	8 cups water
garlic	Seasoned flour
1 bottle Riesling	8 cups cooked linguine
Juice of 1/2 lemon	Tarragon Cream Sauce

Have the butcher cut front legs and neck from the rabbits; save this for the stock. Cut rest of each rabbit down backbone, each with a saddle and hind leg connected. These four pieces are ready for the marinade. Combine corn oil and next 7 ingredients, and mix well. Place the four rabbit pieces in the marinade, and marinate rabbit overnight. Place front legs and neck into Dutch oven with one large carrot. Add 8 cups water, and cook for about 45 minutes to make rabbit stock; set aside. Remove rabbit from stock and from marinade. Shake all rabbit pieces with seasoned flour, and bake in oven at 375° for about 45 minutes or until golden brown. Serve rabbit on hot linguine, and top it with Tarragon Cream Sauce.

Tarragon Cream Sauce:

2 cups rich rabbit sauce	1 tablespoon sugar
2 cups heavy cream	2 cups strained
2 tablespoons country	marinade
Dijon mustard	3 tablespoons blond
2 tablespoons diced	butter roux
fresh tarragon leaves	

Combine all ingredients, except roux, in large saucepan; bring to a boil, and cook for 30 minutes. Stir in blond roux, and cook until mixture is thickened. Serve hot.

Yield: 4 servings
James Graham

Chicken Fried Venison Strips

2 pounds (¹/₂-inch-thick)
   venison steaks
¹/₂ teaspoon salt
¹/₂ teaspoon red pepper

2 eggs
¹/₂ cup milk
3 cups oil
2 cups all-purpose flour

Cut venison steaks into ¹/₄-inch strips; sprinkle with salt and red pepper; refrigerate for 2 hours to marinate. Beat together eggs and milk; set aside. Heat the oil in a large skillet over medium heat. Remove meat from refrigerator; dip each strip in egg mixture, and then dredge through flour, coating well. Shake off excess flour, and fry in hot oil until golden brown.

Yield: 6 servings
Sonny Aymond

Sonny's Smothered Squirrel

2 squirrels, cut into
   bite-size pieces
Salt to taste
Pepper to taste
¹/₄ cup oil
1 cup chopped onion

¹/₂ cup chopped bell
   pepper
¹/₄ cup chopped celery
1 tablespoon minced
   fresh garlic
5 cups water

Sprinkle salt and pepper over meat. In a large cast-iron pot over high heat, add the oil, and heat until hot. Add the squirrel meat, and brown on all sides. Add the onion, bell pepper, celery, and garlic. Cook and stir 5 minutes, or until onions are transparent. Stir in the water, cover, and bring to a boil for 10 minutes. Reduce the heat and continue cooking 1 hour or until meat is tender. Serve over hot cooked rice.

Yield: 4 servings
Sonny Aymond

Pork Stuffed with Turkey & Smoked Sausage

1 whole pork loin
2 tablespoons seasoning salt
4 ounces ground turkey
1/3 cup chopped onion
1/3 cup chopped bell pepper
1/3 cup chopped celery
4 ounces Cajun Country smoked sausage
1 pound thick slab bacon
2 large onions, julienned
1 cup beef stock or ham stock
8 ounces apple juice frozen concentrate, thawed
3 Granny Smith apples, cored and sliced
Cornstarch and water (mixed)

If pork loin is not already sliced in half, do so using a very sharp knife; set aside. Mix seasoning salt, ground turkey, onion, bell pepper, and celery. Grind sausage in a food processor, and add to turkey mixture; mix well. Stuff pork loin with stuffing; tie with butcher string, and wrap with bacon. Roast on rack on sheet pan until internal temperature reaches 170°. Roasting temperature should be 325°. After roast has cooked, pour off bacon grease from roasting pan, and place in a medium saucepan over medium heat. Add onions and caramelize. Then add stock, apple juice concentrate, and apples. Thicken with cornstarch mixture. Let the roast rest at room temperature for 20 minutes. Slice roast, and serve warm sauce over it.

Yield: 10 servings

Bill Bell

You can add 1 teaspoon of fresh thyme to stuffing mixture, if desired.

secretsecretsecretsecretsecretsecretsecretsecretsecretsecretsecretsecretsecret

Richard's Cajun Country Sausage from Louisiana makes this recipe special.

BRONZE—1990

Scallopini Acciuche (Veal Medallions in Anchovy Sauce)

1 cup butter, divided
24 (4-ounce) veal
  medallions
13 ounces anchovies
2 tablespoons crushed
  garlic
¼ cup chopped green
  onions
2 tablespoons crushed
  oregano
2 tablespoons crushed
  almonds
3 cups white wine

In a medium skillet, melt 2 tablespoons butter. Add veal, and sauté until cooked medium rare. Remove veal, and add anchovies. Cook until dark brown (burnt); then add garlic, green onions, oregano, almonds, white wine, and remainder of butter. Add veal, and let liquid reduce for about 5 minutes. Serve immediately.

Yield: 10 servings
Brian Blanchard

secretsecretsecretsecretsecretsecretsecretsecretsecretsecretsecretsecretsecret
You must "burn" the anchovies. It changes the flavor completely.

Zydeco Cowboy Stew

½ cup vegetable oil
3 pounds beef debris
1 onion, chopped
1 bell pepper, chopped
6 cloves garlic, sliced
Zatarain's Creole
  Seasoning to taste
1 quart water
Onion tops, chopped
Roux
1 (6-ounce) can Rotel
  sauce

In black pot on medium heat, heat the oil, and add all debris (which consist of beef liver, cow tongue, kidney, beef heart, mary guts and tripe). Let cook for 45 minutes; then add onion, bell pepper, garlic, and seasoning, and cook for another 30 minutes; Add water and onion tops; cook for 15 minutes. Add roux and Rotel sauce, and cook on medium heat for 15 minutes to thicken.

Yield: 4 servings
Michael Chaisson C.W.C.

Serve on an 8-inch plate over rice; top with Louisiana Gold Pepper Sauce.

secretsecretsecretsecretsecretsecretsecretsecretsecretsecretsecretsecretsecret
This is a real country Cajun dish. You must use a black iron pot, Zatarain's Creole Seasoning, and Louisiana Gold Pepper Sauce. You will really feel the spirit of the meal if you listen to Clifton Chenier's Zydeco music while preparing this stew.

Osso Buco Milanaise

1 (3- to 4-pound) veal
  shanks, cut into 4
  pieces
9 tablespoons butter
4 tablespoons olive oil
1 carrot, chopped
1 onion, chopped
5 cloves garlic,
  chopped
1 bell pepper, chopped
6 ounces mushrooms,
  quartered

4 tablespoons flour
¾ cup dry vermouth
2 cups tomato sauce
2 quarts veal stock
Thyme to taste
Bay leaf to taste
Oregano to taste
Sweet basil to taste
Salt to taste
Pepper to taste

Brown veal shanks in Dutch oven in butter and olive oil until brown. Add carrot, onion, garlic, bell pepper, and mushrooms; sauté until tender. Add flour, and mix well. Deglaze pan with dry vermouth, tomato sauce, and veal stock. Add seasonings, and cook in the oven for 1½ hours.

Yield: 2 servings
Gilbert Decourt

Serve with rice.

Veal Sweetbreads with Nantua Sauce

GOLD—1984

2 pounds veal
   sweetbreads
5 pounds live crawfish
Flour
Egg wash
Breadcrumbs
2 cups butter, divided

1 onion, chopped
1 pound fresh
   mushrooms, chopped
1 quart heavy cream
Salt to taste
White pepper to taste
Red pepper to taste

Nantua is a small town in France. It claims to be the crawfish capital of the world—but we know better.

Bring a pot of salty water to a boil. Add sweetbreads, and cook for 5 minutes. Remove sweetbreads, discard liquid, and cover sweetbreads with a pan to remove excess moisture. In another stockpot, bring 2 quarts water to a boil. Add crawfish, and cook for 5 minutes. Remove crawfish from pot, and peel; set meat aside. Put all the shells back into pot, and cook until liquid is reduced to 1 quart. Strain and set stock aside. Remove any membranes from sweetbreads. Cut into medallions. Dredge membranes in flour, egg wash, and breadcrumbs. Sauté medallions in 1 cup butter until brown on both sides. Drain on paper towels. In a saucepan melt remaining 1 cup butter. Add onion, mushrooms, and seasonings; cook for 2 minutes. Add 1 quart stock and heavy cream, and cook until sauce is reduced. Add veal sweetbreads and crawfish meat. When warm, place medallions on plate, and top with sauce.

Use less cream in sauce.

Yield: 4 servings
Joseph Gonsoulin

Serve with steamed broccoli, cauliflower, and carrots in a shallot butter.

secretsecretsecretsecretsecretsecretsecretsecretsecretsecretsecretsecretsecret
The crawfish add to this dish, as does the way the veal is cooked. It's a New Orleans style of pan sauté called panéed.

BRONZE—1993

While working for Ruth Chris' Restaurants, Joseph combined quality meat with ingredients he learned to love from Latin America. Voila, this recipe, a wonderful contrast of colors, textures, and temperatures.

Tournedos Salsa

4 pounds center-cut beef tenderloin	1 pint whipping cream
Salt to taste	4 threads of saffron
Black pepper to taste	1 pound fresh mushrooms, sliced
White pepper to taste	6 ounces smoked salmon, julienned
Cayenne pepper to taste	Black Bean Puree
3 pounds fresh salmon bones and trimmings	Salsa

Cut tenderloin into 2-ounce portions. Lightly season with salt and peppers. Refrigerate. Place salmon bones and trimmings in a stockpot with enough water to cover. Bring to a boil. Reduce heat, and simmer for 3 hours. Strain stock; set aside. Pour whipping cream into a small saucepot, and bring to a boil. Once cream is reduced by half, remove from heat, and add saffron. Stir until cool. Mix cream and saffron with fish stock. Bring to a light boil, and add mushrooms and smoked salmon; keep warm. Grill tenderloin medallions until medium rare. To serve, place 3 tablespoons of Black Bean Puree on serving plate. Arrange medallions over puree. Ladle cream sauce with salmon and mushrooms over medallions, and top with 1 tablespoon of Salsa.

Black Bean Puree:

1 pound dried black beans	2 jalapeño peppers, seeded and minced
10 garlic cloves, diced	3 to 4 tablespoons olive oil
1 onion, chopped	10 cups chicken stock
2 celery ribs, chopped	
1 carrot, chopped	

Soak black beans overnight. In a medium stockpot sauté garlic, onion, celery, carrot, and jalapeños in olive oil for 10 minutes. Drain black beans, and add them to stockpot; stir in chicken stock. Reduce heat to low, and simmer until beans are tender, about 2 hours. Reserve 2 cups of beans for salsa, and then puree the rest of the bean mixture in a food processor.

Salsa:

2 cups black beans	2 jalapeño, seeded and diced
4 garlic cloves, diced	2 teaspoons fresh lime juice
2 pounds red tomatoes, seeded and diced	4 tablespoons chopped cilantro
6 tablespoons finely diced red onion	Salt and pepper to taste
4 tablespoons finely diced red bell pepper	

(Continued on next page)

Tournedos Salsa (continued)

Toss together 2 cups of black beans with garlic, tomatoes, red onion, bell pepper, jalapeño, lime juice, and cilantro. Season to taste; set aside.

Yield: 10 servings
Joseph Gonsoulin

Brandied Tenderloin Medallion

1 pound angel hair pasta	1 cup fresh mushroom, sliced
1½ pounds beef tenderloins, cut in 2-ounce medallions	¾ cup chopped green onions
3 teaspoons cracked black pepper	½ cup beef stock or beef broth
⅔ cup brandy, divided	¼ teaspoon salt
4 tablespoons butter	⅛ teaspoon cayenne pepper
	¼ cup whipping cream

Cook angel hair pasta as directed on package; rinse, set aside. Sprinkle medallions with cracked black pepper. Pound lightly. Place in bowl. Add 2 tablespoons of brandy. Let marinate in refrigerator for 30 minutes. In a large skillet melt butter over medium heat for 1 minute. Remove from heat. Lay medallions in skillet. Return to heat. (Caution: Brandy may flame; if this happens, cover for 10 to 15 seconds to extinguish.) Remove cover; cook until medium-rare, turning once. Remove medallions, and place on platter in warm oven. Turn heat to high in same skillet, and add mushrooms, green onions, beef stock, salt, and cayenne pepper. Cook on high heat 5 minutes. Add remaining brandy and whipping cream. Cook 3 more minutes or until thick. Place medallions on angel hair pasta, and pour brandy cream sauce on top.

Yield: 4 to 6 servings
Donald R. Hebert

Crustless Quiche Florentine

Use reduced fat or fat-free cheeses; use lean meat or replace meat with vegetables; use skim milk or egg substitute.

2 cups cooked meat (chicken, shrimp, or Canadian bacon)
1 (10-ounce) package frozen chopped spinach, thawed and drained
2 cups (8-ounces) shredded sharp Cheddar cheese
1/2 cup finely chopped onion
1 1/2 cups milk
1 cup ricotta or dry-curd cottage cheese
3/4 cup Bisquick
3 eggs
1/4 cup grated Parmesan cheese
1 teaspoon salt
1/8 teaspoon pepper

Heat oven to 350°. Lightly grease 11x7-inch baking dish. Combine meat, spinach, cheese, and onion. Spoon into prepared dish. Combine remaining ingredients and blend with electric mixer until smooth. Pour over mixture in baking dish. Bake 50 to 55 minutes, or until knife inserted in center comes out clean. Let stand 5 minutes before serving.

Yield: 8 servings
Lynn Epstein, LDN, RD

Serve with fresh fruit and mimosas.

Pork Loin on Pumpkin Sauce

1 (3-pound) pork loin
Salt to taste
Coarsely ground black
 pepper to taste
Oregano leaves to taste
Sweet basil leaves to
 taste
Fresh garlic to taste
2 tablespoons peanut
 oil
Pumpkin Sauce
Toasted pumpkin seeds
 (optional)

Cut the pork into one 1½-inch cut, with the bone, fat, and sinew removed. Season the pork with salt, pepper, oregano leaves, sweet basil leaves, and fresh garlic. Sauté pork in peanut oil for approximately 10 minutes, turning the meat occasionally. Remove and keep warm. Pour some of the hot Pumpkin Sauce onto a plate. Slice pork loin about ¼ inch thick, and arrange in a half circle on the sauce. If desired, sprinkle with toasted pumpkin seeds. Garnish with vegetables of your choice.

Pumpkin Sauce:
2 tablespoons peanut
 oil
2 tablespoons finely
 diced shallot
½ tablespoon finely
 diced garlic
½ tablespoon finely
 diced ginger
Lemon zest
1 small bay leaf
4 anise seeds
Pinch of finely diced red
 chile
1 cup coconut milk
½ cup pork stock
5 ounces ripe pumpkin
 (boiled until soft, 8-
 10 minutes)
Salt to taste

Heat oil in pan, and sauté shallots and garlic for 2 minutes or until light brown. Add ginger, lemon zest, bay leaf, anise seeds, and red chile; sauté another 2 minutes. Add coconut milk and pork stock; bring to a boil. Reduce heat, and simmer 4 minutes. Add pumpkin and salt to taste; cook 8 minutes. Discard bay leaf, pour mixture in blender, and process 2 minutes. Strain and set aside.

Yield: 6 servings
Ken Koval

Cajun Pork Jambalaya Acadie

Roy has been cooking all kinds of jambalayas for more than 30 years. Many folks get the basic jambalaya technique wrong from the beginning.

Vegetable oil
1 ½ pounds pork, diced
2 ounces pork tasso, minced
6 ounces Cajun smoked sausage, thinly sliced
2 medium onions, diced
1 large green bell pepper, diced
1 jalapeño, deseeded and minced
1 small turnip, peeled and grated
3 tablespoons minced fresh garlic
1 (10¾-ounce) can cream of mushroom soup
1 tablespoon Worcestershire sauce
1 ½ teaspoon Try Me Tiger Sauce
1 tablespoon salt
1 tablespoon black pepper
2 teaspoons cayenne pepper
1 teaspoon granulated onion
1 teaspoon granulated garlic
7 cups beef stock (low sodium)
1 tablespoon Kitchen Bouquet
3 cups long-grain rice
1 cup thinly sliced green onions
2 tablespoons minced parsley

Using a 6- to 8-quart thick black pot with lid, pour just enough vegetable oil to cover the bottom of the pot, and heat. Once the oil is hot, add the diced pork, and brown well. Stir often to brown evenly. Add the tasso and sausage, and cook for 5 more minutes, stirring well. Add the onion, bell pepper, jalapeño, turnip, and garlic, mixing well. Cook on medium until the onions are transparent. Add the cream of mushroom soup, Worcestershire, Tiger sauce, salt, black pepper, cayenne pepper, granulated onion, and granulated garlic; stir well, and simmer for 5 minutes. Add the beef stock, and bring to a boil. Taste the liquid; it should be a little salty and peppery, and the meat flavors should prevail. Allow the mixture to boil for 3 minutes. Add the Kitchen Bouquet, and stir. Measure 3 cups of rice, and wash with cold water; drain well. Add rice to the simmering mixture, and stir for 1 minute so rice does not stick. Allow this to simmer for about 15 minutes or until rice has absorbed all the stock except for ½ inch over the level of rice and meat. Lower heat; add green onions and parsley, and stir well. Cover with lid, and allow to cook for 20 minutes on very low fire. After 15 minutes, stir with folding action, cover, and allow it to finish cooking. The finished product should have absorbed all the liquid but remain moist. This goes well with cole slaw.

Yield: 4 to 6 servings
Roy Lyons

secretsecretsecretsecretsecretsecretsecretsecretsecretsecretsecretsecret

For the best possible dish, brown the meat well, allowing it to stick. Add 2 to 4 tablespoons cold water, just not allowing it to burn. You'll see a brown gravy beginning to develop. Allow for water evaporated as many times as you like or until the rich-brown, thick gravy is apparent.

Jambalaya

1½ pounds cubed beef
1 pound boneless
  chicken breasts,
  cubed
⅔ pound hot smoked
  sausage links, sliced
1 cup chopped onion
⅓ cup chopped celery
¼ cup oil
4 cups long-grain rice,
  uncooked

3 bay leaves
4 teaspoons salt
7 cups chicken broth
2 teaspoons cayenne
  pepper
¼ cup chopped green
  onions
2 tablespoons chopped
  parsley

Sauté beef, chicken, sausage, onion, and celery in oil until tender and partially caramelized. Add remaining ingredients, and cook on medium-high heat until broth is absorbed in rice. Stir, reduce heat to low, and cook covered for 20 minutes. Let stand covered for 10 minutes.

Yield: 10 to 12 servings
William Menard

Menard and his old buddy "Doc" Danterive would sit outside and cook this jambalaya in a big black iron pot. What started with just a few folks watching football would end up being a neighborhood reunion.

Cajun Chili

3 pounds ground meat
1 large onion, chopped
6 (4-ounce) cans
  tomato juice
1 can Rotel tomatoes
2 tablespoons cumin

2 tablespoons chili
  powder (or to taste)
Tony Chachere's Creole
  Seasoning to taste
3 tablespoons instant
  corn mesa mix or
  cornstarch

Brown meat with onion. Pour off grease. Add next 3 ingredients, and simmer 30 minutes. Correct seasoning. Add chili powder and Creole seasoning. Add corn mesa to thicken.

Yield: 4 servings
William M. O'Dea C.E.C., A.A.C.
Serve in bowls with grated Cheddar cheese on top.

Use low-fat ground beef.

secretsecretsecretsecretsecretsecretsecretsecretsecretsecretsecretsecret
Rotel tomatoes and Tony Cachere's Creole Seasoning make this Cajun.

Smoked Beef Tenderloin Diablo

4 tablespoons butter
½ tablespoon cracked
  black pepper
2 tablespoons chopped
  green onions

1 pound rare smoked
  beef tenderloin, sliced
4 tablespoons brandy
2 cups Bordelaise Sauce
4 ounces crawfish tails

Heat butter. Add cracked black pepper, green onions, and sliced beef. Sear meat on both sides. Flame with brandy. Add Bordelaise Sauce and crawfish tails to tenderloin. Cook to desired doneness and serve.

Bordelaise Sauce:
5 quarts rich veal or
  beef stock
1 large onion,
  quartered
12 whole black
  peppercorns
2 tablespoons minced
  garlic
3 tablespoons tomato
  paste

2 tablespoons
  Worcestershire sauce
1 tablespoon seasoning
  salt
¾ cup dry red wine
1 tablespoon Kitchen
  Bouquet (optional)
2 teaspoons salt
5 tablespoons white
  roux
¼ pound chilled butter

Combine all ingredients except white roux and butter. Bring to boil, and simmer for 1 hour. Thicken sauce by adding white roux. Once thickened, add butter; stir till butter has melted. Strain sauce through fine mesh sieve.

Yield: 2 servings
Patrick Mould C.E.C.

Smoke whole beef tenderloin seasoned with liberal amounts of seasoning salt, garlic, Worcestershire sauce, and Tabasco in a conventional smoker over your choice of hardwood. The tenderloin is considered rare when the internal temperature of the meat reaches 120° on a meat thermometer.

Cajun Fettuccini

8 ounces butter or margarine
1 medium onion, chopped
1 medium green bell pepper, chopped
1 medium red bell pepper, chopped
1 stalk celery, chopped
1 cup all-purpose flour
1 quart heavy cream
3 ounces Parmesan cheese or Velveeta cheese
5 ounces andouille or smoked sausage, coarsely chopped
8 ounces cooked ham or chicken breast, finely chopped
4 ounces tasso, finely chopped
Tony Chachere's Creole Seasoning to taste
1 ½ cups finely chopped green onions with tops, divided
½ cup chopped parsley, divided
1 pound fettuccine noodles

Melt butter over medium heat. Sauté onion, bell pepper, celery until limp (about 5 minutes). Add flour, and stir for a few minutes, do not over brown. Add heavy cream, cheese, and meats, stirring constantly. Add seasoning to taste, ¾ cup green onions with tops, and ¼ cup parsley. Turn heat off. Be sure to stir constantly because cheese will burn fast. Cook 1 pound fettuccine noodles according to directions. Drain well. Place noodles on plate; top with sauce and green onions and parsley.

Yield: 10 servings
William M. O'Dea C.E.C., A.A.C.

secretsecretsecretsecretsecretsecretsecretsecretsecretsecretsecretsecret
Tony's Chachere's Creole Seasoning, Savoies Tasso, Savoies Andouille Sausage, and Hormel Ham are all recommended for a Cajun treat.

SILVER—1986

Use light
mayonnaise.

Veal Supreme

1 ½ pounds veal fillet	1 cup Mock Hollandaise
8 tablespoons unsalted	Sauce
butter	3 cups almonds,
1 cup Curry Sauce	toasted and sliced

Cook veal in butter 1 minute; add Curry Sauce, and bring to a boil. Add Mock Hollandaise Sauce. Sprinkle with toasted almonds on top of each serving.

Curry Sauce:

1 medium onion,	½ cup chicken broth
minced	½ cup pineapple juice
1 stalk celery, chopped	Salt to taste
1 clove garlic, crushed	⅛ teaspoon ground
¼ cup butter	white pepper
1 tablespoon curry	1 cup flaked coconut
powder	2 apples, cored, peeled,
¼ cup unsifted flour	and diced

Sauté vegetables in butter until limp. Add curry powder; sauté 1 minute. Blend in flour; slowly add chicken broth and pineapple juice, and heat until thickened. Add salt and pepper to taste. Add coconut and apples. Cover and simmer 1 hour stirring occasionally. Strain.

Mock Hollandaise:

¼ cup butter	1 ¼ cups mayonnaise
½ lemon juice	

Melt butter over low heat. Beat in lemon juice. Beat in mayonnaise. Heat and beat 2 minutes longer.

Yield: 6 servings
William M. O'Dea C.E.C., A.A.C.

Real Hollandaise Sauce may be used in place of Mock Hollandaise.

Oven-Stuffed Pork Chops

4 (1-inch-thick) center
   cut pork chops
1/2 cup chopped onion
1/3 cup chopped green
   bell pepper
1/3 cup chopped red bell
   pepper
1/2 pound fresh ground
   pork
1/2 pound fresh ground
   beef
1 teaspoon salt

1 teaspoon ground
   white pepper
1 teaspoon paprika
1/2 teaspoon ground red
   pepper
2 tablespoons
   breadcrumbs
1/4 teaspoon
   Worcestershire sauce
1 teaspoon salt
1 teaspoon ground red
   pepper
1 teaspoon paprika

On a flat surface using a sharp knife, make a pocket inside of pork chop lengthwise. Place the onion and bell peppers in a food processor, and puree. In a large bowl combine the pureed vegetables, ground pork, ground beef, and the next 6 ingredients, mixing well. Divide the mixture into 4 equal amounts and overstuff each pork chop. Place stuffed pork chops in a 9x12-inch baking dish. Mix salt, red pepper, and paprika; sprinkle over pork chops. Place in a 400° preheated oven, and bake 40 minutes or until browned.

Yield: 4 servings
Chris Oncale

These chops are easy to make — and very tasty.

BRONZE—1989

Veal à la Eli

¹/₈ teaspoon salt
¹/₈ teaspoon white
  pepper
¹/₈ teaspoon red pepper
¹/₂ teaspoon paprika
1 pound veal fillet
Vegetable cooking
  spray
3 tablespoons butter
¹/₃ cup tasso, finely
  chopped

1 cup sliced fresh
  mushrooms
¹/₂ cup sliced green
  onions
1 ¹/₂ cups whipping
  cream
1 cup lump crabmeat
¹/₂ teaspoon paprika
Salt and pepper to taste

Mix salt and next 3 ingredients in small bowl. Sprinkle over veal on both sides. Spray with vegetable spray. Place on hot grill, and cook 5 minutes; turn, cook 4 minutes, remove from grill, and place on plate. Keep warm. In a medium skillet on high heat, combine butter and next 3 ingredients; cook 10 minutes, shaking skillet constantly. Add whipping cream, and cook an additional 10 minutes or until cream starts to thicken. Add crabmeat, and cook until thoroughly heated. Do not overcook. Place fillets on plates. Spoon tasso-crabmeat cream sauce over top.

Yield: 4 servings
Enola Prudhomme

secretsecretsecretsecretsecretsecretsecretsecretsecretsecretsecretsecretsecret

Using tasso makes it hard to use other seasoning because tasso verses other seasonings. Always add tasso first, cook for a few minutes, taste, and adjust seasoning.

Pork Chops with Gingersnap Gravy

1 teaspoon paprika
½ teaspoon salt
½ teaspoon ground
white pepper
½ teaspoon ground
black pepper
⅛ teaspoon dry
mustard
⅛ teaspoon celery seed
⅛ teaspoon ground
coriander
⅛ teaspoon ground
nutmeg

2 tablespoons oil
1 pound lean pork
chops, cut ¼ inch
thick
1 cup chopped onion
½ cup chopped green
bell pepper
½ cup chopped red bell
pepper
1½ cups beef stock or
water, divided
5 gingersnap cookies
3 cups hot cooked rice

Combine the first 8 ingredients in a small bowl. Mix well, and sprinkle over both sides of pork chops. Add the oil to a large skillet, and place over medium heat. Add pork chops, and cook 2 minutes on each side, turning often. Add the onion, bell peppers, and 1 cup of the stock; cook and stir 15 minutes. Add the remaining stock and gingersnaps. Cook and stir until gingersnaps are dissolved. Serve over hot cooked rice.

Yield: 6 servings
Enola Prudhomme

BRONZE—1988

Bryan learned to prepare this dish during a sejour at an Italian restaurant in Lafayette owned by a Sicilian family.

Add garlic, if desired, and skip dessert. Don't try low-fat mayonnaise.

Vitello Tonnato (Veal with Tuna Sauce)

1 (5-pound)boneless veal shoulder	Tuna Sauce
1 rib celery, chopped	Powdered parsley
1 carrot, sliced diagonally	1 lemon, peeled and sliced
2 tablespoons chopped Italian parsley	2 tablespoons tiny capers
Sea salt to taste	2 anchovy fillets
Cayenne to taste	Carrot slices
White pepper to taste	6 ripe olives

Braise the veal in water with the celery, carrot, and parsley. Add sea salt, cayenne, and white pepper to taste. Simmer in this broth for 1½ hours or until tender. Then remove veal, and allow to cool ½ hour. Slice and then arrange on a chilled platter and refrigerate. When chilled, cover the veal slices completely with the Tuna Sauce, making ripple patterns in the sauce with a spatula. Garnish sauce with powdered parsley, lemon slices, capers, anchovies, carrot slices, and ripe olives. Cover with plastic film, and chill at least 3 hours before serving.

Tuna Sauce:

1 pound fresh albacore tuna	1 cup mayonnaise
White wine	½ cup dry white wine
4 tablespoons chopped white onion	Cayenne pepper to taste

Poach tuna quickly in saucepan in small amount of white wine. Remove from pan, and gently flake. Blend the tuna, onion, mayonnaise, ½ cup white wine, and cayenne in a food processor.

Yield: 6 servings
Bryan Richard

Feature this dish at a outdoor luncheon. Serve it with Cortese di Gavi white wine, garlic bread, and a spinach or Swiss chard salad.

secretsecretsecretsecretsecretsecretsecretsecretsecretsecretsecretsecret
When Bryan completes this dish, he must taste it so it fits all qualifications of Acadiana life — hot, sexy, tasty, and fast. The freshness and underdoneness of the tuna is very important.

Spit-Roasted Stuffed Pork Lafayette

1 (3-pound) pork loin	2 tablespoons orange
12 garlic cloves,	zest
roasted	2 tablespoons canola
5 peppercorn mix	oil
(freshly cracked)	Salt to taste
2 red onions, peeled	2 tablespoons cayenne
and finely minced	pepper
2 cups golden raisins	5 peppercorn mix
(soaked in orange	2 tablespoons minced
juice)	rosemary leaves
1 cup figs, chopped	Steen's cane syrup
2 cups French bread	
cubes moistened with	
6 beaten eggs	

Trim any surplus fat from the pork. Flatten it out with a meat mallet. Insert garlic cloves with the tip of a boning knife, and season with the peppercorns; set aside. Mix onion and next 4 ingredients together. Spread this evenly over the meat, leaving a 2-inch border nearest you. Roll up the meat starting at the far end, and secure with fine string. Combine the canola, salt, cayenne, and peppercorn mix with minced rosemary into a paste. Rub this over the roast, and rotisserie for 1 hour and 20 minutes, brushing occasionally with the pan juices and cane syrup.

Yield: 6 servings

Bryan Richard

Serve with baked Louisiana yams, petit pois with pearl onions and mushrooms, and warm yeast rolls.

This recipe was developed to serve at a Senate luncheon hosted by John Breaux to benefit the American Cancer Society.

The rotisserie method eliminates much of the fats, and rosemary enhances the digestion of the fats.

GOLD — 1990

Flank Louisiane

2½ pounds flank steak
1 cup water
6 teaspoons Worcestershire
4 teaspoons white wine Worcestershire
¼ cup lime juice
1 cup peanut oil
5 teaspoons all-purpose seasoning
2 teaspoons parsley
2 teaspoons chopped green onions

Marinate flank steaks in water and next 5 ingredients for 4 to 24 hours. Grill steaks. Slice very thinly, and arrange on Dressing. Add Sauce, and garnish with parsley and green onions.

Dressing:

4 ounces salt-free butter
½ cup sliced mushrooms
½ cup diced onion
1 shredded carrot
1 stalk celery
1 bell pepper, diced
1 clove garlic
10 ounces shrimp
1 teaspoon basil
1 teaspoon all-purpose seasoning
2 teaspoons parsley
2 ounces fresh spinach
¼ loaf French bread, cut in cubes
1 egg, beaten

In a skillet melt butter and sauté mushrooms, onion, carrot, celery, bell pepper, and garlic. Dice shrimp and add to mixture. Add basil, all-purpose seasoning, parsley, and spinach. When shrimp are cooked, add French bread and beaten egg. Mix thoroughly.

Sauce:

4 teaspoons salt-free butter
½ cup water
1 teaspoon all-purpose seasoning
½ cup beef stock or au jus
½ cup red wine
1½ teaspoons flour
½ pint whipping cream

Melt butter in saucepan, and add water. Combine seasoning and au jus. Bring to a boil. After reducing liquid to desired thickness, add wine, and return to boil. Lower fire and simmer. Add flour a little at a time, using a wire whip. When butter and liquid join together, add whipping cream to sauce.

Yield: 10 servings
Joseph Schreiber C.W.C.

secretsecretsecretsecretsecretsecretsecretsecretsecretsecretsecretsecretsecret
Home prepared all-purpose seasoning consists of 14 herbs and spices: white pepper, black pepper, red pepper, onion powder, garlic powder, thyme, chili powder, dill, paprika, mustard, basil, tarragon, oregano in a 10% salt mixture.

Applewood-Smoked Javelina (Wild Boar) Sausage with Tomato-Apple Chutney

3 pounds ground javelina meat or pork	Cumin to taste
1½ pounds ground apple-smoked bacon slab	Thyme to taste
	Salt to taste
	Garlic granulated to taste
Red pepper to taste	Chili powder to taste
Black pepper to taste	Tomato-Apple Chutney

Grind javelina and bacon together. Mix seasonings and meat mixture in mixing bowl, and then fry a little at a time to adjust seasonings. Once seasonings are correct, stuff mixture into cleaned hog casings. Smoke slowly over mesquite and applewood until desired temperature. Serve with Tomato-Apple Chutney.

Tomato-Apple Chutney:

2 large ripe tomatoes, chopped	½ cup water
2 large cooking apples, chopped	¼ cup raisins
	Salt to taste
1 cup brown sugar	Red pepper to taste
¾ cups red wine vinegar	1 stick cinnamon
1 onion, finely chopped	1 tablespoon pickling spice

In a saucepan combine all ingredients, and bring to a boil. Reduce heat. Simmer uncovered for 45 minutes until thickened.

Yield: 10 servings
Britt Shockley

Crushed-Pepper-Coated Crab-Stuffed Loin of Pork

6 pounds pork loin
2 cups butter
1 cup diced mushrooms
¹/₂ cup diced red bell pepper
1 cup diced onion
1 bunch green onions, chopped
2 teaspoons chopped garlic
1 cup cream
¹/₂ pound Monterey Jack cheese, shredded
¹/₄ cup chopped jalapeños
¹/₂ cup white wine
¹/₂ loaf soft French bread, cubed
2 pounds white crabmeat
¹/₂ cup crushed red pepper
Black pepper to taste

Spiral cut pork loin. Pound about ¹/₄ inch thick; set aside. To prepare stuffing, melt butter, and sauté mushrooms, bell pepper, onion, and garlic until tender. Add cream and cheese, and cook 5 minutes. Add jalapeño peppers and wine. Season to taste. Add soft bread to thicken; fold in crabmeat. Spread stuffing on pork evenly. Roll and tie with butcher string. Sprinkle with crushed red pepper and black pepper to taste. Roast in oven at 325° until center reaches 150°. Serve with sauce.

Pork-Veal Demi-Glaze:
3 pounds veal bones
3 pounds pork bones
1 pound leeks
¹/₂ pound carrots
¹/₂ pound celery
2 gallons water
2 ounces tomato paste
2 bay leaves
1 tablespoon thyme
1 tablespoon basil
1 tablespoon whole black peppercorns
Red pepper to taste
Blond roux

Roast veal bones, pork bones, leeks, carrots, and celery until browned. Place in stockpot with 2 gallons water and tomato paste. Tie up a cheesecloth sachet bag with bay leaves and next 4 ingredients; add to pot. Reduce liquid by half. Adjust seasoning. Thicken with blond roux.

Yield: 10 servings
Britt Shockley

SILVER—1990

Oyster-Stuffed Pork Loin with Apple Cider Cream Sauce

1 (6-pound) boneless pork loin
½ cup oil
2 cups chopped onion
2 cups chopped celery
2 cups chopped green bell pepper
5 dozen oysters (reserve liquid)
10 cloves garlic, minced
2 tablespoons seafood base
1 pint heavy cream, as needed
Seasoned breadcrumbs
Crushed red peppercorns
Black pepper
Thyme
Salt
Apple Cider Cream Sauce

Spiral cut pork loin until it is shaped rectangular and about ½ inch thick. In saucepan, brown onion, celery, and bell pepper. Add oysters, garlic, and oyster liquid. Cook 3 to 4 minutes. Add seafood base and heavy cream. Cook 5 minutes. Add breadcrumbs to thicken. If too thick, add more cream and adjust seasonings. Cool. Spread mixture evenly over pork. Start at one end rolling up pork to give a jellyroll effect. Tie with butcher's knot. Roll in crushed red peppercorns. Bake at 350° until brown and tender. Cut into medallions. Place Apple Cider Cream Sauce on serving plate. Place medallions on top of sauce.

Apple Cider Cream Sauce:
4 tablespoons butter
4 tablespoons flour
1 quart heavy cream
3 cups apple cider
Red pepper
Salt
Sage
½ cup Calvados brandy

Melt butter. Add flour until blond roux forms. Stir in mixture of heavy cream and apple cider; reduce by half. Stir in red pepper, salt, and sage to taste. Cook until thickened, stirring frequently. Add brandy to mixture. Bring to a gentle simmer. Serve.

Yield: 10 servings
Britt Shockley

The sauce is the secret to this recipe. It combines sweet apple cider and tart brandy, which the judges described as "awesome" and "incredible." The sauce can be used on any type of pork dish.

Veal Riverfront

4 ounces of angel hair pasta
2 cups egg wash (2 eggs and 1 cup milk)
2 (2-ounce) veal medallion
1 cup flour
4 tablespoons butter, divided
3 large shrimp
1 tablespoon diced tomatoes
1 tablespoon sliced mushrooms
1 teaspoon garlic
1 teaspoon fresh basil
1 teaspoon fresh thyme
1 teaspoon seasoning salt
1 ounce of brandy
1 ounce of sherry
Parsley to garnish

Boil angel hair pasta until tender; set aside. In a small pan or bowl combine the egg wash. Place the veal in the egg wash, making sure that both sides have absorbed the mixture somewhat; then place veal in flour. Sauté each side of the veal for 30 seconds in 2 tablespoons butter. In a small skillet, sauté the shrimp, tomato, mushrooms, garlic, herbs, and seasoning salt in the remaining butter, until the shrimp are cooked. Add the brandy and sherry. Let simmer for 1 minute. Place the pasta in the middle of a serving platter; add veal around sides. Top with shrimp mixture. Garnish with parsley. Serve.

Yield: 2 servings
Chris Sogga

Roasted Hazelnut Grouse

6 ounces boned grouse	1 large poblano pepper, chopped
1 ounce chicken forcemeat	Cumin powder to taste
1 large red bell pepper, chopped	Chili powder to taste
1 large yellow bell pepper, chopped	Granulated garlic to taste
2 large jalapeño peppers, chopped	Red pepper to taste
1 large chile pepper, chopped	Salt to taste
	1 ½ ounces deer tenderloin
	Curry Sauce

Split grouse down backside, leaving one leg in. Mix chicken forcemeat with peppers and seasonings; set aside. Sear tenderloin over high heat until rare; set aside. Open grouse, and spread pepper stuffing evenly over meat. Place tenderloin in center, and roll and tie with butcher's string. Roast at 325° until center reaches 140°. Serve with Curry Sauce.

Curry Sauce:

1 tablespoon butter	1 apple, peeled and chopped
4 teaspoons curry powder	⅓ cup chopped celery
15 ounces chicken stock	2 tablespoons coconut
½ cup chopped onion	4 teaspoons chutney
½ cup chopped carrots	1 clove garlic, minced
1 tomato, peeled and chopped	1 bay leaf
	Seasoning salt to taste
	Thyme to taste

Melt butter in saucepan. Add curry powder. Add chicken stock, onion, carrots, tomato, apple, celery, coconut, chutney, garlic, bay leaf, seasoning salt, and thyme. Bring to boil and reduce heat. Simmer uncovered for 60 minutes or until vegetables are very tender. Place half of mixture at a time in blender, and mix until smooth.

Yield: 10 servings
Britt Shockley

secretsecretsecretsecretsecretsecretsecretsecretsecretsecretsecretsecret

The different games make this a regional favorite. Yet the unusual application of layering the pepper stuffing and tenderloin atop the boned grouse, and rolling it all together, arouses even local taste buds.

Chicken Bayou Teche

1 small fryer
1 large red bell pepper,
  chopped
1 large yellow bell
  pepper, chopped
½ cup chopped
  jalapeño peppers
1 large yellow onion
½ pound butter

1 pound ground beef
1 pound crabmeat
Salt to taste
Pepper to taste
Granulated garlic to
  taste
Cracker meal
Sauce

Bone fryer, leaving one leg in and all meat intact; set aside. Sauté peppers and onion in butter until soft. Brown ground beef, and place with peppers. Fold in crabmeat and seasonings. Thicken with cracker meal and cool. Place filling in chicken, and roll up tight. Tie with butcher's string. Roast at 350° until internal temperature reaches 160°, about 40 minutes. To serve, slice and cover with sauce.

Sauce:

½ cup butter
2 tablespoons all-
  purpose flour
16 ounces heavy cream
Garlic to taste
Cayenne pepper to
  taste

Black pepper to taste
Basil to taste
Thyme to taste
1 pound diced bacon
1 (14-ounce) can Rotel
  tomatoes

Melt butter. Add flour, and cook to form a blond roux. Add cream and seasonings. Sauté bacon until crisp, and add to sauce. Add Rotel tomatoes, and reduce until thick. Adjust seasonings to taste.

Yield: 10 servings
Britt Shockley
You can use large chicken breasts instead of whole fryer.

BRONZE—1991

Pollo alla Granchio
(Seafood-Stuffed Chicken Breast)

½ pound crabmeat
½ pound shrimp
1 cup grated Parmesan
 cheese
1 tablespoon crushed
 oregano
1 tablespoon crushed
 marjoram
1 cup béchamel cream,
 divided
1 tablespoon salt

1 tablespoon pepper
1 teaspoon crushed
 garlic, divided
5 (8-ounce) chicken
 breasts
½ cup butter
1 cup heavy cream
½ cup chicken stock
1 teaspoon cracked
 black pepper
¼ cup green onions

In large bowl mix crabmeat, shrimp, Parmesan cheese, oregano, marjoram, ½ cup béchamel cream, salt, pepper, and ½ teaspoon garlic. Pound chicken breasts until ¼ inch thick. Spread stuffing over chicken; then roll breasts, securing with a wood pick. Sauté chicken in butter until golden brown. Discard excess oil. Add heavy cream, ½ teaspoon garlic, chicken stock, cracked pepper, green onions, and ½ cup béchamel cream. Simmer until sauce thickens.

Yield: 5 servings
Brian J. Blanchard

SILVER—1992

Pollo Ricotta e Spinaci

½ pound crawfish
½ pound spinach
½ cup ricotta cheese
½ tablespoon crushed
 garlic
¼ cup grated Parmesan
 cheese
1 tablespoon oregano

5 (8-ounce) boned
 chicken breasts, split
½ cup white wine
½ cup béchamel cream
½ cup basil leaves
¼ cup pine nuts
¼ cup heavy cream

Place crawfish, spinach, ricotta cheese, garlic, Parmesan cheese, and oregano in bowl; mix well. Stuff chicken breasts, and bake at 350° for 20 minutes. Put wine, béchamel cream, basil, pine nuts, and heavy cream in skillet. Sauté until mixture thickens; then pour over stuffed breasts.

Yield: 5 servings
Brian J. Blanchard

Using only half a breast, stuff the meat at the wide end and shape the piece to look like a teardrop.

Stuffed Pheasant with Morel Sauce

½ cup chopped celery	¼ teaspoon black
½ cup chopped onion	pepper
½ cup chopped	¼ teaspoon garlic
mushrooms	powder
1 (6-ounce) boneless	¼ teaspoon sweet basil
chicken breast	2 yellow bell peppers,
4 ounces tasso	julienned
2 ounces bacon	3 ounces chopped
1 ounce ham	spinach
2 ounces pork fat	2 carrots, julienned
2 eggs	3 whole pheasants,
¼ teaspoon salt	boned

Sauté celery, onion, and mushrooms. Grind vegetables with chicken, tasso, bacon, ham, and pork fat. Grind three times, each time using smaller hole. Mix ground meat with eggs, salt, pepper, garlic powder, and sweet basil. Spread small amount of mixture on 3 pieces of wax paper. Top each with julienned pepper. Mix 1 cup of meat mixture with spinach. Spread small amount of spinach mixture on top of each pepper layer. Place carrots in center of each; roll each layered mixture, and freeze. Take rolls from freezer, and stuff pheasants. Tie each, and cook at 350° until 160° internal. Slice and serve with Morel Sauce.

Morel Sauce:

1 ounce dried morel	2 cups glaze (made
mushrooms, soaked	from pheasant and
in water	veal bones)
	1 cup Madeira wine

Drain morels, chop if needed, and add to glaze. Add Madeira wine. Serve.

Yield: 10 servings
Patrick Breaux

GOLD 1989

Chicken Ballottine with Bell Pepper Coulis

4 ounces chicken	Pinch salt
2 ounces bacon	2 egg yolks
2 ounces smoked ham	3 spinach leaves
1 ounce tasso	3 (7-ounce) boneless
½ cup (total) chopped	chicken breasts,
onion, bell pepper,	flattened
and celery	2 red bell peppers
Pinch red pepper	2 yellow bell peppers
Pinch black pepper	Season to taste

Blend first 8 ingredients in a food processor. Add egg yolks and spinach leaves. Put mixture into seasoned chicken breasts. Roll chicken. Place chicken in aluminum foil, and twist ends. Bake at 325° until done. For sauce, cook peppers on open flame until charred. Peel, seed, and puree separately. Season to taste. Slice chicken. Place a little of each sauce on plate. Place sliced chicken on top of sauce.

Yield: 4 to 6 servings
Patrick Breaux

Roti Chicken

1 whole chicken, cut	1 large onion, diced
into pieces	1 bell pepper, diced
All-purpose seasoning	1 cup chicken or beef
to taste	broth
½ cup vegetable oil	½ cup green onions
1½ tablespoons sugar	½ cup parsley

Season chicken. Cook oil and sugar over medium heat in a heavy saucepan. Add chicken as soon as sugar browns. Add onion and bell pepper; cook for 10 minutes. Add broth. Cook another 10 minutes or until chicken is done. Top with green onions and parsley.

Yield: 4 to 6 servings
Patrick Breaux

This is a tasty recipe that's simple to prepare. It's great served with rice and a tossed salad.

Oriental-Stuffed Chicken Breast

4 (6-ounce) boneless
  chicken breasts
1 quart commercial
  Chinese marinade
4 ounces diced tasso
1 onion, diced
1 bell pepper, diced
1 garlic clove, minced
2 cups diced cabbage
Seasoning to taste

4 ounces ground veal
2 ounces ground beef
4 ounces ground
  chicken
1 egg
5 ounces poached
  spinach
Ginger and Red Wine
  Sauce

Marinate breasts for 4 hours in marinade. Sauté tasso, onion, bell pepper, garlic, and cabbage. Season and chill. When chilled, add to ground meats and run through grinder twice. Add egg to mixture. Wrap chicken breasts around stuffing, and tie with a string. Put in rotisserie, and cook until done. Serve Ginger and Red Wine Sauce over chicken.

Ginger and Red Wine Sauce:

$1/2$ cup chopped shallots
3 ounces butter
1 teaspoon peppercorns
$1/2$ teaspoon garlic

1 cup red wine
$1/4$ teaspoon grated
  ginger
3 cups glace de viande

Sauté shallots in butter. Add peppercorns and garlic. Add wine, and reduce to half. Add ginger and glace de viande. Simmer for 60 minutes. Strain and serve over chicken.

Yield: 4 servings
Patrick Breaux

Duck Strudel

Joe got this recipe from Gordon Marr, Executive Chef Washington Hilton Hotel who spent several weeks touring Louisiana to learn Cajun/ Creole cuisine. The seasonings and duck made it a natural to please the local palate.

½ cup diced green onions
1 cup chopped bok choy
½ cup finely diced carrots
¼ cup finely diced red bell pepper
¼ cup finely diced yellow bell pepper
¼ cup bean sprouts
¼ cup bamboo shoots
1 pound boneless, skinless duck, julienned

Fresh ginger to taste
Fresh garlic to taste
2 teaspoons peanut oil
2 teaspoons soy sauce
2 teaspoons hoisin (adjust to taste)
2 teaspoons rice vinegar
Black pepper to taste
White pepper to taste
Red pepper to taste
1 package phyllo dough
4 ounces melted butter

Sauté vegetables and duck with ginger and garlic in peanut oil. Vegetables should remain crunchy. Season to taste. Mix soy, hoisin, and rice vinegar. Toss with vegetables and duck to coat. Put mixture in a strainer to cool. Excess liquid should be eliminated before assembly of strudel. Place one layer of phyllo dough on a damp cloth; lightly butter. Place another piece of dough on that. Repeat so that you have 4 or 5 layers. Put duck mixture along edge of dough. Roll dough jelly roll fashion. Brush with melted butter. Bake at 450° for 15 to 20 minutes (just until golden brown). Slice and serve on Plum Sauce.

Plum Sauce:

1 quart commercial Oriental plum sauce
1 pound frozen raspberries

Rice vinegar to taste
1 ounce plum wine
Hoisin to taste
Arrowroot

Mix first 5 ingredients. Thicken with arrowroot. Strain to eliminate seeds. Serve on plates topped with duck.

Yield: 4 servings
Joseph Broussard

Oriental plum sauce right out of the jar could be used, but if time allows, it's better if it can be modified with the above ingredients.

Chicken Breasts Lombardy

6 boned chicken
  breasts, skinned and
  quartered
All-purpose flour
1 cup melted butter or
  margarine, divided
Salt to taste
Pepper to taste
1 ½ cups sliced
  mushrooms

¾ cup Marsala wine
½ cup chicken stock
½ teaspoon salt
⅛ teaspoon pepper
1 ½ tablespoons butter
  or margarine
½ cup shredded Fontina
  or mozzarella cheese
½ cup grated Parmesan
  cheese

Substitute no-fat margarine for butter. Use low-fat cheeses.

Flatten each chicken breast between sheets of waxed paper to ⅛-inch thickness. Dredge chicken lightly with flour. Place 4 pieces at a time in 2 tablespoons melted butter in a medium skillet. Cook over low heat 3 to 4 minutes on each side or until golden brown. Place chicken in a greased 13x9x2-inch baking dish, overlapping edges. Sprinkle with salt and pepper. Repeat procedure with remaining chicken. Reserve drippings in skillet. In a small skillet, sauté mushrooms in ¼ cup melted butter until tender; drain. Sprinkle evenly over chicken. Stir wine and chicken stock into drippings in medium skillet. Simmer 10 minutes, stirring occasionally. Stir in salt, pepper, and 1 ½ tablespoons butter. Spoon about a third of the sauce evenly over chicken, reserving remainder. Combine cheeses, and sprinkle over chicken. Bake at 450° for 10 to 12 minutes. Place under broiler 1 to 2 minutes or until lightly browned. Serve with reserved sauce.

Yield: 8 servings
Joseph Broussard

Turkey breast may be substituted for chicken. Instead of Marsala wine, ¾ cup white wine plus 1 tablespoon brandy may be used.

secretsecretsecretsecretsecretsecretsecretsecretsecretsecretsecretsecretsecret
The Fontina cheese gives this dish its special flavor.

Chicken à la Bonne Femme

Substitute olive oil instead of butter; eliminate bacon.

1 whole chicken,
   quartered
Vegetable oil
3 potatoes, peeled and
   sliced
½ pound bacon, cut
   into 1-inch slices
1 onion, sliced

1 bell pepper, sliced
½ cup butter
Creole seasoning to
   taste
2 cups water
½ bunch green onion
   tops, chopped

Pan fry chicken until done; set aside. Pan fry potatoes; set them aside. Pan fry bacon; set aside. Sauté onion and bell pepper in butter in large skillet until transparent. Add chicken, potatoes, bacon, and Creole seasoning to taste. Add water, and simmer for 20 minutes. Garnish with onion tops, and serve with rice.

Yield: 4 servings
Michael Chaisson C.W.C.

secretsecretsecretsecretsecretsecretsecretsecretsecretsecretsecretsecretsecretsecret
You need to use Zatarain's Creole Seasoning to get the right taste.

Chicken Breast Bordelaise

2 boneless chicken
   breasts
3 ounces all-purpose
   flour
2 ounces butter
1 ounce olive oil
1 ounce bacon
6 ounces fresh
   mushrooms, sliced

Thyme to taste
1 bay leaf
1½ cups red Bordeaux
   wine
5 ounces butter,
   softened
Salt and pepper to taste

Dust chicken breasts in flour, and sauté in butter and olive oil until brown. Drain excess oil; set chicken aside. To the skillet, add chopped bacon, mushrooms, thyme, and bay leaf. Sauté until mushrooms are tender. Deglaze pan with wine, and reduce by half; then add soft butter, mixing well with a whisk. Add salt and pepper. Put chicken back in the sauce, and cook for 4 minutes. Place each chicken breast on a plate, and top it with sauce.

Yield: 2 servings
Gilbert Decourt

Serve with fettuccine or spinach fettuccine.

Stuffed Chicken Anaclaire

SILVER—1990

4 (6-ounce) boned
  chicken breasts
Salt to taste
Pepper to taste
½ cup chopped onion
1 rib celery, chopped
¼ cup chopped green
  bell pepper
¼ cup chopped red bell
  pepper
¼ pound lump
  crabmeat

¼ pound cooked baby
  shrimp
1 egg
Breadcrumbs
Pernod to taste
1 pint chicken stock
1 pint heavy cream
1 cup unsalted butter
½ cup all-purpose flour
½ cup white wine
2 mushrooms, sliced
  and sautéed
Season to taste

Pound and season chicken breasts; set aside. Sauté onion, celery, and peppers; place in a large bowl. Add lump crabmeat, shrimp, egg, and breadcrumbs. Add Pernod. Set aside for 1 hour or until firm. Cut chicken breasts in half. Put half of large kitchen spoon of stuffing in each chicken breast, and roll up. Hold together with a wooden pick. Bake at 375° for 30 minutes. Keep warm. Bring chicken stock and heavy cream to a boil. Make a roux of butter and flour. Add to stock mixture; whisk together until creamy. Add white wine and sautéed mushrooms. Season to taste. Spoon sauce on top or under chicken, and serve hot.

Yield: 10 servings
Wayne Jean

Louisiana Campfire Grilled Stuffed Chicken Breasts

1 slice white bread, diced	1 egg white
1 tablespoon cream	Poultry seasoning to taste
4 ounces diced Granny Smith apples	Salt to taste
½ ounce raisins	Pepper to taste
½ ounce chopped roasted pecans	2 (5-ounce) chicken breasts
	Cranberry Coulis

Soak bread in cream. Add apples and next 6 ingredients; mix well, and set aside. Skin, butterfly, and debone chicken breasts, except wing bone. Clean wing bone well. Place stuffing inside, and grill. Serve with Cranberry Coulis.

Cranberry Coulis:

1 cup chicken stock	Salt to taste
8 ounces fresh cranberries	White pepper to taste
¼ cup Grand Marnier	Cayenne pepper to taste

Heat stock. Add cranberries, and simmer on low for about 10 minutes. Add Grand Marnier, and cook 1 more minute. Add seasonings, and then puree. Strain, adjust seasoning, and hold until needed.

Yield: 2 servings
Kenneth Koval

Use chicken bones to make stock for cranberry coulis.

Cone Hat Stuffed Pasta

½ pound all-purpose flour	Pinch of salt
3 egg yolks	Stuffing
2 whole eggs	Sauce

Measure flour into bowl. Make a well in center, and add egg yolks, whole eggs, and salt. Thoroughly mix egg into flour. Form dough into a ball. Chill for 30 minutes; then roll out to desired thickness. Cut out a 3x3-inch square. Fill and seal with stuffing and shape into hat. Boil and hold till serving. Serve with sauce.

Stuffing:

1 medium onion, chopped	Sweet basil to taste
1 teaspoon minced garlic	Oregano to taste
2 ounces butter	Salt to taste
1 pound chicken, skinned and ground	Black pepper to taste
	1 egg yolk
	2 ounces chicken stock

Sauté onion and garlic in butter until brown. Add chicken, sweet basil, oregano, salt, and pepper. Cook for 2 minutes. Remove from heat, and transfer to mixing bowl. Add egg yolk, and moisten with chicken stock. Blend well.

Sauce:

3 tablespoons olive oil	2 tablespoons finely chopped fresh basil
2 tablespoons finely chopped shallots	1 tablespoon finely chopped fresh oregano
2 tablespoons finely chopped fresh parsley	1 small bay leaf
1 tablespoon minced garlic	Salt to taste
8 large roma tomatoes, peeled, seeded and chopped	Black pepper to taste
	3 ounces cream

Heat oil in iron skillet over low heat. Cook shallots, parsley, and garlic for 2 minutes. Do not brown. Add tomatoes, basil, oregano, bay leaf, salt, and pepper. Bring to boil; then reduce heat. Simmer, partially covered, for 30 minutes. Run through fine sieve twice. Stir in cream, and serve with pasta.

Yield: 6 to 8 servings
Kenneth Koval

One of Ken's childhood friends was of Italian Catholic descent. Meals with his friend's family always included pasta — with special pasta dishes on Sunday. This dish is Ken's special pasta, reminiscent of a bishop's hat.

Wild Turkey Breast Lafayette

1 (8- to 10-pound)
  turkey
6 ounces ground pork
  fat
Liver from bird
Salt to taste
2 ounces diced onion
2 ounces diced celery
4 ounces sliced
  mushrooms

3 ounces butter
3 eggs, beaten
5 ounces heavy cream
Salt to taste
Pepper to taste
Poultry seasoning to
  taste
Sauce

Debone turkey. Cook bones to make stock for sauce. Save skin, keeping it as whole as possible. Keep breast chilled. Puree dark meat, pork fat, and liver with salt in vertical cutter or high-powered blender. Keep all ingredients and equipment as cold as possible. Sauté onion, celery, and mushrooms in butter for 3 minutes. Drain well. Mix egg and cream with meat until fully absorbed. Add seasonings and sautéed vegetables. Mix well. Keep chilled until needed for breast roll. Cut breast in half; then butterfly from left to right in center of breast. Spread dark meat mixture on breast. Wrap in a roll with reserved skin. Roast at 325° until breast reaches 155° internal temperature. Let rest 10 minutes before slicing. Slice and serve with sauce.

Sauce:

2 ounces finely diced
  shallots
2 ounces finely diced
  mushrooms
2 ounces dry vermouth
16 ounces turkey stock

2 tablespoons
  cornstarch
Water
Salt to taste
Pepper to taste

Brown shallots in pan drippings, and add mushrooms. Sauté 1 minute. Deglaze with dry vermouth. Add stock, and simmer for 10 minutes. Thicken with cornstarch and water. Strain and adjust seasonings.

Yield: 10 servings
Kenneth Koval

Stir Fry Chicken & Three Peppers

2 pounds chicken
   tenders, cut into bite-
   size pieces
1/4 cup soy sauce
1/2 cup dry sherry or rice
   wine vinegar
2 teaspoons ground
   ginger
1/2 teaspoon Chinese
   red pepper
1/2 teaspoon sesame oil
2 tablespoons peanut
   oil

2 red bell peppers,
   julienned
2 green bell peppers,
   julienned
2 yellow bell peppers,
   julienned
1 purple onion, sliced
1 tablespoon garlic,
   minced
2 tablespoons
   cornstarch
1/4 cup water

Reduce oils
to reduce fat.

Marinate chicken with soy sauce, sherry, ginger, red pepper, and sesame oil for 20 minutes to 2 hours ahead of time. When the time comes to cook, heat wok on high heat until very hot. Remember: hot wok, hot oil, food won't stick. When oil is hot, add chicken (reserving marinade), and stir fry for about 5 minutes or until browned nicely. Push chicken on sides of wok. Add peppers, onion, garlic, and reserved marinade. Mix all together, and stir fry for 3 to 5 minutes. Mix cornstarch and water. Add to wok. Cook 2 to 3 minutes longer.

Yield: 4 servings
Lonnie B. Pope, Jr.

Serve over hot rice or Chinese rice noodles.

secretsecretsecretsecretsecretsecretsecretsecretsecretsecretsecretsecret

Many Acadians like Chinese food, but don't care for the vegetables. That's why this one has basic Cajun vegetables.

Turkey Avec Ecrevisse

5 pounds turkey breast
Marinade
Crawfish Stuffing
6 slices bacon

Sauce
Cranberry/Mango relish
(fresh)

Flatten turkey, place in marinade, and marinate for 24 hours. Remove turkey from marinade, reserving marinade. Fill turkey with stuffing. Roll turkey up, and bind together with bacon. Cook turkey for 20 minutes in oven at 325°; save drippings for sauce. Grill turkey to 155°, while basting with marinade. Serve with sauce and Cranberry/Mango relish.

Marinade:
1 cup peanut oil
½ cup liquid smoke
1 cup white wine
Worcestershire

1½ teaspoons fresh
garlic
3 teaspoons all-purpose
seasoning

Mix all ingredients well. Use to marinate turkey.

Crawfish Stuffing:
4 ounces salt-free
butter
½ cup sliced
mushrooms
½ cup diced onion
1 carrot, shredded
1 bell pepper, diced
1 stalk celery, chopped
1 clove garlic, minced
2 teaspoons flour
1 cup water
¼ cup crawfish fat

12 ounces crawfish
2 ounces spinach
1 teaspoon fresh basil
1 teaspoon all-purpose
seasoning
2 teaspoons parsley
2 teaspoons green
onions
½ cup pepper cheese
¼ loaf French bread,
cubed

In a skillet, melt butter, and sauté mushrooms, onion, carrots, bell pepper, celery, and garlic. Add flour and blend in. Add water and crawfish fat. Dice crawfish, and add to mixture. Add fresh basil, seasoning, parsley, green onions, and pepper cheese. When crawfish are cooked, add French bread, and mix thoroughly.

Sauce:
6 teaspoons butter
3 teaspoons flour
2¼ cups milk
1 cup Chardonnay
1 teaspoon special all-
purpose seasoning

4 teaspoons drippings
from turkey
¾ cups heavy cream
1 teaspoon green
onions
1 teaspoon parsley

(Continued on next page)

Turkey Avec Ecrevisse (continued)

Melt butter, and whisk in flour. Cook, stirring for 1 minute. Remove from heat, and stir in a third of the milk until smooth. Add the remaining milk, wine, and seasoning. Add drippings from turkey. Bring to boil, stirring constantly; cool for 5 minutes. Whisk in the cream, and heat thoroughly. Then stir in green onions and parsley.

Yield: 10 servings
Joseph Schreiber C.W.C.

All-purpose seasoning is a mixture of 12 herbs and spices with a 10% salt content.

SILVER—1988

Grilled Quail Acadie

1 tomato, chopped, peeled, and seeded	1 teaspoon Tiger sauce
1½ cups chicken stock	1 teaspoon Tabasco
1 teaspoon garlic	1 teaspoon seasoning salt
1 teaspoon Lea & Perrin's Sauce	White roux
	6 quail

Combine first 7 ingredients together, and thicken up with a white roux; set aside, and keep warm. Grill quail, and serve with sauce.

Yield: 6 servings
Patrick Mould

Garlic Grilled Chicken

3 tablespoons red wine vinegar	3 tablespoons chopped garlic
6 tablespoons Cajun Power Garlic Sauce	2 tablespoons Tabasco
4 teaspoons seasoning salt	1 cup olive oil
	8 chicken breasts, trimmed

Combine first 5 ingredients in a food processor, and blend on medium speed. Slowly add olive oil until all is incorporated. Marinate chicken breasts in mixture at least 2 hours. Grill chicken, preferably over hardwood, for 5 to 6 minutes on each side, depending on size of chicken breast.

Yield: 8 servings
Patrick Mould C.E.C.

Poulet à l'Intrigue

3 pounds boneless chicken breast (skin on)	Stuffing
	Hickory chips
Marinade	Sauce

Marinate chicken breast for 24 hours. Place stuffing under skin of chicken. Bake chicken for 15 minutes at 350°; then take chicken breast, and smoke lightly for 10 minutes with hickory chips. Remove to serving plate, and add sauce.

Marinade:

1 cup peanut oil	4 teaspoons all-purpose seasoning
1 cup hickory barbecue sauce	½ cup lime juice
1 cup water	1 teaspoon minced fresh garlic
6 teaspoons white wine Worcestershire	2 teaspoons chopped onion

Mix all ingredients well; pour over chicken.

Stuffing:

4 ounces salt-free butter	1 clove garlic, chopped
10 ounces sausage	1 teaspoon all-purpose seasoning
½ cup chopped onion	1½ cups chicken stock
½ cup chopped celery	5 ounces eggplant
1 red bell pepper, chopped	2 teaspoons parsley
1 shredded carrot	2 teaspoons chopped green onions
½ cup chopped mushrooms	½ loaf French bread, cubed

In a large skillet, melt butter, and sauté sausage. Then add onion, celery, pepper, carrot, and mushrooms. Next add garlic, seasoning, and chicken stock. Next add diced eggplant (cooked and drained) with parsley and green onions. Turn off heat, and add French bread.

Sauce:

6 teaspoons butter	1 teaspoon parsley
3 teaspoons flour	1 teaspoon green onions
2¼ cups milk	
1 cup Chardonnay	¼ pound andouille sausage
1 teaspoon all-purpose seasoning	¼ pound pecans, chopped
2 cups chicken stock	
¾ cups whipping cream	

Melt butter, and whisk in flour. Cook by stirring for 1

(Continued on next page)

Poulet à l'Intrigue (continued)

minute. Remove from heat; stir in milk until smooth. Add wine, seasoning, and chicken stock. Bring to a boil, stirring constantly; simmer for 5 minutes. Whisk in cream, bring to temperature, and add parsley, green onions, andouille, and pecans.

Yield: 10 servings
Joe Schreiber C.W.C.

Baked Breast of Duck

10 duck breasts	**10 provolone cheese**
1 pound tasso	**slices (thin)**
	Strawberry Cream Sauce

Pound both sides of duck breasts with meat cleaver. Place two slices of tasso on duck and one slice of provolone cheese on top of the tasso. Roll duck; then place one toothpick through the front of the breast and another through the bottom of breast. Bake for 20 minutes at 350°. When ducks are done, slice at 45 degree angle. Pour Strawberry Cream Sauce on bottom of plate. Place duck on sauce with duck slices overlapping one another. Serve.

Strawberry Cream Sauce:

1 quart heavy whipping cream	**$\frac{1}{2}$ cup fresh strawberries, sliced**
1 tablespoon chicken base	**1 teaspoon granulated onion**
1 tablespoon roux	**1 teaspoon granulated garlic**
$\frac{1}{2}$ cup frozen strawberries with syrup	

While duck is cooking, pour heavy cream in a 2-quart saucepan on high heat. Add chicken base when cream starts to boil. Stir in roux, and simmer for 5 minutes on low heat. Add remaining ingredients. The color will change to light red. Simmer sauce until the ducks are done.

Yield: 10 servings
Chris Sogga

Louisiana-Style Chicken Fricassee

3½ tablespoons lard
1 (3 to 3½ pound)
  fryer, cut up
Flour for dredging plus
  1 tablespoon
2 cups chopped onion
2 cups chopped green
  bell pepper
1¼ teaspoons salt
1¼ teaspoons freshly
  cracked black pepper
1 bay leaf, crushed
¼ cup finely minced
  fresh parsley
½ teaspoon thyme

1¼ teaspoons cayenne
  pepper
1 teaspoon minced
  garlic
1 teaspoon
  Worcestershire sauce
Tabasco to taste
10 young white turnips
  or new potatoes,
  peeled
10 cloves garlic, minced
½ to 1 quart rich
  chicken stock
Hot cooked rice
Chopped green onions

In a large heavy stockpot, melt the lard over medium heat. Dust the chicken parts with flour, and brown on all sides. Remove to a platter. Add 1 tablespoon flour to make roux. When roux is desired color, add onion and pepper. Stir in chicken, salt, and next 10 ingredients. Add rich chicken stock to make a gravy. Cook on low heat for 45 minutes to 1 hour. Stir every few minutes to distribute the seasonings. Adjust the seasoning, if necessary. Spoon chicken and gravy over cooked rice, and top with chopped green onions. Serve immediately.

Yield: 4 servings
Bryan Richard

secretsecretsecretsecretsecretsecretsecretsecretsecretsecretsecretsecret

At the turn of the century, Creole and Acadian cooks prepared chicken this way, with onions, lots of peppers, water, and the Creole Bouquet Garni — parsley, bay leaves, and thyme.

GOLD—1991

Chris gives credit to his parents for his pastry talent. They owned Koonie's Bakery in Opelousas for 28 years. He began working with them when he was 8 years old.

Cajun Crunch in a Cloud

2 dozen assorted day-
  old muffins
2 cups sugar
8 ounces chocolate
  chips
2 (6-ounce) boxes
  instant chocolate
  pudding or pie filling
1 (11¾-ounce) box
  cheesecake mix (omit
  crust)
2 cups chopped pecans
2 cups whole milk
2 cups heavy cream
1 teaspoon butter-
  flavored extract
½ cup water
2 cups chocolate syrup
Cloud

Crumble muffins in a large bowl. Blend in sugar, chocolate chips, pudding, cheesecake mix, and pecans. Combine milk, cream, butter-flavored extract, and water. Add to crunch mixture. Place in 9x9x2-inch casserole dish. Bake in a vat of water at 350° for 40 minutes or until firm. Top with chocolate syrup. Cut into equal squares, and place on cloud mixture. Serve hot and enjoy.

Cloud:
1 quart heavy cream
2 cups sugar
2 teaspoons vanilla
  extract

Blend cream, sugar, and vanilla until thick. Spoon onto dessert plates.

Yield: 10 servings
Chris Oncale

Peach Cobbler

1 cup buttermilk	2 cups chopped
1 cup heavy cream	peaches
2 tablespoons	4 tablespoons
margarine	cornstarch
1 cup peach juice	¼ cup water
1 cup sugar	Batter

In a 4-quart heavy saucepan, on high heat, combine buttermilk, cream, margarine, peach juice, and sugar. Bring to boil, and add peaches. Combine cornstarch and water. Add to boiling mixture. Remove from heat. Set aside. Spray 13x9x2-inch pan with nonstick spray. Layer two-thirds of batter in pan. Add two-thirds of filling over batter. Layer remaining batter over filling. Bake at 425° for 25 minutes. After removing cobbler from oven, layer the remaining filling over cobbler for extra flavor.

Batter:

2 cups biscuit mix	½ cup peach juice
½ cup sugar	½ cup buttermilk
½ cup heavy cream	

In a medium bowl add biscuit mix, sugar, cream, peach juice, and buttermilk. Mix for 1 minute.

Yield: 8 servings
Chris Oncale

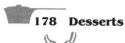

BRONZE—1991

Pears Poached in Red Wine, Filled with Fruit Bavarian

1 cup red wine	1 clove
¼ cup lemon juice	1 ounce crème de cassis
1 vanilla bean	10 pears, peeled
½ cup sugar	Fruit Bavarian
½ ounce pear liqueur	1 pint mango coulis

Bring wine, lemon juice, vanilla bean, sugar, pear liqueur, clove, and crème de cassis to boil. Add pears. Simmer until done. Refrigerate overnight. Core pears, and pipe Fruit Bavarian into center. Chill. Cut and serve over mango coulis.

Fruit Bavarian:

½ ounce gelatin	1¾ cups heavy cream
½ cup cold water	¼ pound assorted fresh
1 pint vanilla cream, heated	fruit slices

Dissolve gelatin in cold water. Add to hot vanilla cream. Whip heavy cream. Fold cooled vanilla into whipped cream. Add fruit. Stuff cream into pears.

Yield: 10 servings
Patrick Breaux

Basil Buttermilk Pie

2 eggs	½ teaspoon lemon zest
1 cup sugar	2 cups buttermilk
¼ cup flour	1 10-inch unbaked pie
2 tablespoons butter	shell
1 tablespoon chopped basil	

Combine eggs, sugar, flour, butter, basil, lemon zest, and buttermilk in a bowl. Beat until blended. Pour mixture into pie shell. Bake at 425° for 10 minutes. Reduce temperature to 325°, and bake for 25 minutes.

Yield: 8 servings
Jessica Broussard

Serve chilled with fresh strawberries.

Kiwi & Spice Cake

½ cup melted butter
3 eggs
¾ cup sugar
¼ cup brown sugar
1 teaspoon cinnamon
1 teaspoon nutmeg
½ cup sour milk (½ cup milk, 1 teaspoon baking soda, and 1 teaspoon vinegar)

2 cups flour
1 teaspoon vanilla extract
2 cups kiwi, diced and cooked with 1 cup sugar
Mousse
Sauces

Mix all cake ingredients except kiwi. At last moment, add kiwi. Put in greased Bundt pan, and bake at 350° until wood pick tests clean. To serve, pipe Mousse in center, and serve cake with one or all the Sauces.

Mousse:

4 teaspoons gelatin
¼ cup cold water
2 cups sugar
2 cups water

2 cups heavy cream, whipped
1 teaspoon vanilla extract

Dissolve gelatin in water. Dissolve sugar in two cups of water in saucepan. Add gelatin. At room temperature, add whipped cream. Chill. Let firm. Pipe into center of dessert.

Sauces:

1 pint mango
1 pint blackberries

1 pint raspberries
Sugar to taste

Make each sauce by puréeing fruit, adding sugar to taste, and running through a sieve.

Yield: 10 servings
Patrick Breaux

Blueberry-Nut Cheesecake

¼ **cup unbleached flour**	**Filling**
½ **cup brown sugar**	**8 ounces blueberry pie**
½ **cup Butter Flavored**	**filling**
Crisco	½ **cup chopped pecans**
½ **cup chopped pecans**	

Combine flour and next 3 ingredients; reserve ½ cup of mixture. Press the remaining into a 9-inch springform pan. Bake at 350° for about 15 minutes. Add filling, and bake for 35 to 40 minutes. Top with blueberry topping, reserved crust mixture, and pecans. Bake an additional 10 minutes.

Filling:

3 (8-ounce) packages	⅓ **cup sour cream**
cream cheese	**2 tablespoons blueberry**
1 cup sugar	**schnapps**
3 eggs	

Cream cream cheese; add remaining ingredients, one at a time, mixing after each addition. Pour onto baked crust.

Yield: 10 to 12 servings
Jessica Broussard

Callie's Pecan Pie

This recipe was passed down through several generations of Joe's wife's family.

3 eggs	½ **cup sugar**
2 tablespoons melted	**1½ cups dark corn**
butter	**syrup**
2 tablespoons flour	**1½ cups pecan pieces**
¼ **teaspoon vanilla**	**Pie Crust**
½ **teaspoon salt**	

Beat eggs. Blend in butter, flour, vanilla, salt, sugar, and corn syrup. Sprinkle in pecans, and mix gently. Place filling in pie crust, and bake at 425° for 10 minutes; then reduce to 325° for 30 to 40 minutes. Remove from oven, and allow to cool.

Pie Crust:

1½ cups flour	**4 to 6 teaspoons ice**
1 teaspoon salt	**water**
½ **cup shortening**	

Sift flour and salt. Cut in shortening. Add ice water and toss lightly with fork. Roll out on lightly floured surface. Gently place in 8-inch pie pan. Trim and crimp edges.

Yield: 6 to 8 servings
Joseph Broussard

Carrot Cake

2 cups sugar	3 teaspoons cinnamon
2 cups flour	4 eggs
1 teaspoon salt	1 1/4 cups oil
2 teaspoons baking soda	3 cups grated carrot
	Frosting

Mix all dry ingredients. Add eggs, oil, and carrots. Mix well. Pour into 3 (9-inch) greased and floured round pans. Bake at 350° for 30 to 35 minutes. Add frosting when cool.

Frosting:

1/2 cup butter	1 (16-ounce) box confectioners' sugar
1 (8-ounce) package cream cheese	1 teaspoon vanilla
	1 cup chopped pecans

Cream butter and cream cheese. Slowly add half the confectioners' sugar. Mix well after each addition. Add vanilla. Mix in pecans.

Yield: 12 to 16 servings
Jessica Broussard

Bake in a 13x9x2-inch pan and do not frost for a breakfast treat.

This recipe is based on one handed down to Jessica by a great aunt on her mother's side.

A Cajun lives to eat, not eats to live.

Texas Pudding Cake

1 1/4 cups flour	1 (16-ounce) container whipped topping, divided
1/2 cup softened margarine	1 (4-ounce) box instant chocolate pudding
1 cup pecans	1 2/3 cups milk
1 (8-ounce) package softened cream cheese	Pecans
1 cup confectioners' sugar	

Mix flour, margarine, and pecans by hand or on low speed with mixer. Spread mixture in a 13x9x2-inch pan. Bake at 350° for 30 minutes. Allow to cool completely. Cream the cream cheese. Add confectioners' sugar and mix well. Mix 8 ounces whipped topping with cream cheese mixture. Evenly spread half of cream cheese mixture on baked crust. Mix pudding and milk. Spread over cheese layer. Spread remaining cheese mixture on top of pudding. Top with remaining whipped topping. Garnish with pecans.

Yield: 12 to 15 servings
Bernal Thompson C.E.C., C.C.E.

GOLD 1983

GOLD—1993

Feuillantine Con Frutte Fresce

Hazelnut Cookie:

2 cups ground
 hazelnuts
½ cup sugar

½ cup dark corn syrup
6 tablespoons unsalted
 butter

Fruits:

5 pears
1 quart water
Vanilla to taste
½ cup butter

½ pound sugar
1 quart water
10 ounces strawberries
 or raspberries

Crème Anglaise:

1 pound sugar
24 egg yolks

3 quarts milk
Vanilla to taste

Mocha and Chocolate Mousse:

1 quart Crème Anglaise
8 ounces whipped
 heavy cream

2 tablespoons coffee
 extract
10 ounces semi-sweet
 chocolate, melted

Vanilla and Frangelica Mousse:

1 quart Crème Anglaise
1 tablespoon Frangelica
Vanilla to taste

8 ounces whipped heavy
 cream

Caramel Sauce:

30 ounces Crème
 Anglaise
10 ounces caramel
 sauce

10 ounces chocolate
 shavings

To make hazelnut cookies, mix the first 4 ingredients, and bake in the oven for a few minutes. Poach fresh pears in 1 quart water and vanilla; slice them, and caramelize with butter and sugar. Mix with fresh berries, and set aside. To make Crème Anglaise, in a glass or stainless-steel bowl, whip sugar and egg yolks until pale yellow. Temper egg yolk mixture with scaled milk; add vanilla. Heat over double boiler, stirring until mixture coats back of spoon. Make Mocha and Chocolate Mousse by mixing 1 quart Crème Anglaise with whipped cream, coffee extract and melted chocolate. Prepare Vanilla and Frangelica Mousse by mixing Crème Anglaise, Frangelica, vanilla, and whipped cream. Prepare Caramel Sauce by combining Crème Anglaise and caramel sauce (at room temperature). Assemble the dessert in this order: Caramel Sauce on plate, cookie, one of the mousses, fruit, cookie, fruit, the other mousse, and top with cookie and chocolate shavings.

Yield: 10 servings
Gilbert Decourt

Reduced Fat Cream Cheese Cake

2 cups graham cracker
    crumbs
¼ cup granulated sugar
2 egg whites

Filling
Topping
Cinnamon to taste

Preheat oven to 350°. Combine first 3 ingredients, and press on bottom and sides of a 9-inch springform pan. Bake about 5 minutes. Pour Filling into crust. Bake about 30 minutes. Pour Topping over crust. Cook 5 minutes, or until mixture slightly bubbles. Sprinkle cinnamon over top, and bake 2 to 3 minutes to lightly brown cinnamon.

Filling:

1 tablespoon unflavored
    gelatin (dissolved in
    ¼ cup boiling water)
1 (8-ounce) package
    fat-free cream cheese

1 (8-ounce) package
    low-fat cream cheese
½ cup granulated sugar
½ cup egg substitute

Beat gelatin mixture in a large mixing bowl until fluffy and foamy. Add cream cheeses, and beat well. Slowly beat in sugar. Beat in egg substitute and whip until fluffy.

Topping:

1 cup low-fat sour
    cream
¾ cups granulated
    sugar

1 teaspoon pure vanilla
    extract

Combine sour cream, sugar, and vanilla extract; pour over baked filling.

Yield: 12 servings
Lynn Epstein L.D.N., R.D.

Fat-free sour cream is not recommended since it separates when heated.

Lynn based this recipe on a recipe for a cheese pie that her husband found in a biochemistry journal.

Philly Cream Cheese Cake

2 cups graham cracker crumbs	**Filling**
	Topping
½ cup melted butter	**Sliced almonds, roasted**
¼ cup sugar	**Cinnamon**

Preheat oven to 350°. Combine first 3 ingredients, and press on bottom and sides of a 9-inch springform pan. Bake 5 minutes to caramelize sugar. Pour Filling into crust, and bake 30 minutes. Add Topping, and cook 5 minutes, or until mixture slightly bubbles. Sprinkle almonds over top; then lightly sprinkle with cinnamon. Bake 2 to 3 minutes to brown cinnamon slightly.

Filling:

2 (8-ounce) packages cream cheese	**½ cup sugar**
	3 eggs

Soften cream cheese in a large mixing bowl with an electric mixer. Beat in sugar slowly. Slowly beat in eggs, one at a time, until mixture is fluffy. Pour over crust.

Topping:

1 cup sour cream	**1 teaspoon vanilla extract**
¾ cup granulated sugar	

Combine sour cream, sugar, and vanilla extract; pour over baked filling.

Yield: 12 servings

Lynn Epstein L.D.N., R.D.

Bread Pudding with Jack Daniels Sauce

3 (1-pound) loaves stale
  bread
4 cups milk
8 eggs
1 (12-ounce) can
  evaporated milk
½ cup water
¾ cup butter

2 cups sugar
2 tablespoons vanilla
½ teaspoon nutmeg
1 to 2 teaspoons
  cinnamon
1 cup butter (cut into
  pieces)
Sauce

James didn't stop pursuing this recipe until he had it in hand. It's one of those rare jewels.

Cube bread. Set aside in a large mixing bowl. Combine all ingredients except 1 cup butter. Mix well, and pour over bread. Soak bread in milk mixture for 15 minutes. Pour into a 13x9-inch buttered pan. Top bread mixture with cut up butter. Bake at 325° for 60 to 90 minutes, or until pudding mixture has risen 1 inch. Serve warm Sauce over bread pudding.

Sauce:
½ cup sugar
½ cup water

½ cup butter
2 ounces Jack Daniels
  (Black label)

Mix sugar and water until dissolved. Add butter, and simmer until melted. Cook over high heat for 2 minutes. Add Jack Daniels, and simmer for 3 to 5 minutes.

Yield: 24 servings
James Graham

All ingredients should be a room temperature. If using fresh bread, place in oven to make stale.

Cheese Cake

3 (8-ounce) packages cream cheese
4 eggs
1 cup sugar
¼ cup process cheese spread
Crust
Topping

Let cream cheese and eggs come to room temperature in a medium mixing bowl. Add sugar and cheese spread. Beat at low speed for 15 minutes. Pour filling into prepared Crust, and bake at 350° for 20 minutes. Spread Topping evenly over cake, and bake for another 8 minutes. Remove from oven, and cool for 3 hours in the refrigerator.

Crust:

1¼ cups graham cracker crumbs
2 tablespoons melted margarine
2 tablespoons sugar

Combine all ingredients, and mix well. Place in a 9-inch pie plate. With a fork, evenly press mixture around bottom and side of pie plate. Add filling.

Topping:

1 pint sour cream
1½ teaspoons vanilla
2 tablespoons sugar

Make topping by mixing sour cream, vanilla, and sugar in a medium bowl. Beat for 1 minute with a hand mixer. Spread over baked cake.

Yield: 8 servings
Donald R. Hebert

Pecan Nut Sauce

1 (16-ounce) box brown sugar
4 ounces corn syrup
1 cup water
8 ounces chopped pecans
½ cup butter
2 cups heavy cream

Combine brown sugar, corn syrup, and water. Heat until temperature reaches 320°. Add pecans, butter, and cream; remove from heat. Serve warm.

Yield: about 1 quart
Ken Koval

This is great over ice cream or pound cake.

Turtle Cheesecake

2 tablespoons butter
1 cup vanilla wafer
  crumbs
1 cup finely chopped
  pecans
Filling
4 cups caramel cream
3 cups pecan pieces

4 cups chocolate cone
  coating
Bavarian Cream
1 cup pecan-flavored
  chocolate syrup
¼ pound assorted color
  gum paste for roses

*Covering a plain
vanilla cheesecake
with caramel and
pecans then
dipping it in a
chocolate coating
proved to be a
medal-winner for
this chef.*

Mix butter, crumbs, and pecans to form crust in a 9-inch springform pan. Pour filling into pan, and bake at 350° for 60 minutes. Cool and then refrigerate overnight. Cut cake into 10 portions. Spread caramel on top and sides of cake, and roll in pecans. Place in freezer for 1 hour. Dip each portion in warm cone coating, and place on wire rack for chocolate to set. Place ½ cup Bavarian Cream on large dinner plate, and swirl in syrup for marbled effect. Garnish with gum paste roses.

Filling:
4 (8-ounce) packages
  cream cheese
2 eggs
2 cups sugar

1 tablespoon vanilla
1 tablespoon unflavored
  gelatin

Mix cream cheese, eggs, sugar, vanilla, and gelatin. Pour over crust.

Bavarian Cream:
8 egg yolks
2 cups sugar
1 quart heavy cream

1 vanilla bean
1 pint whipped cream

Whip egg yolks and sugar until soft peaks form. Boil cream with vanilla bean. Mix egg mixture and hot cream. Cook on low until it coats back of spoon. Strain and refrigerate. Fold in whipped cream.

Yield: 10 serving
William Menard

A wild turkey hunter from Sunset provided the fresh pumpkin for this recipe.

Pumpkin Cheese Cake Sunset

4 (8-ounce) packages
  cream cheese
2 cups sugar
8 ounces cream
3 eggs
2 egg yolks
Ground cloves to taste
¼ teaspoon salt

½ teaspoon cinnamon
½ teaspoon nutmeg
½ teaspoon ginger
1 tablespoon maple
  extract
10 ounces fresh
  pumpkin
Gingersnap crust

Mix cream cheese and sugar until smooth. Add cream, and mix 1 minute. Mix in eggs and yolks until fully absorbed. Combine spices, extract, and pumpkin. Add to cream cheese. Mix well. Pour on gingersnap crust. Place pan in a water bath, and bake at 390° for 45 minutes. Reduce to 340° and bake for 45 minutes. Turn off oven. Let rest 30 minutes.

Gingersnap crust:
8 ounces ground
  gingersnaps
8 ounces ground
  graham crackers

6 ounces sugar
¾ cup melted butter

Mix crumbs and sugar. Add melted butter. Rub with hands until crust has consistency of wet sand. Press into a springform pan.

Yield: 8 to 10 servings
Ken Koval

For a crisper crust, line springform pan with mixture, and bake at 375° for 6 to 8 minutes.

Bosco Pie

1 (9-inch) deep-dish pie shell
2½ teaspoons melted butter, cooled
4 large eggs
14 tablespoons sugar
1⅛ cups Light Karo syrup
¼ teaspoon salt
1¼ teaspoons Jack Daniels
1¼ teaspoons vanilla extract
1 cup semi-sweet chocolate chips
1¼ cups roasted pecans, chopped

Slightly toast pie shell. Cool to room temperature. In a mixing bowl, lightly beat butter and eggs. Add sugar, Karo syrup, salt, Jack Daniels, and vanilla. Mix well. Fill pie shell half full with mixture. Bake at 350° for 20 minutes or until filling sets. Top with chocolate chips. Spread evenly and level. Add chopped pecan pieces, and spread evenly and level. Pour the remainder of the pie filling over the pecans. Make sure pecans are completely covered. Return to oven, and bake for an additional 20 to 25 minutes. When done, top of pie should be set and have a slight sheen. Cool 30 minutes before serving.

Yield: 4 to 6 servings
Roy Lyons

Serve alone or heat in microwave for a minute and top with your favorite vanilla ice cream.

secretsecretsecretsecretsecretsecretsecretsecretsecretsecretsecretsecret

Roast pecans at 350° for 10 minutes. Stir often, and do not burn. Natural oils will cause pecans to brown and be shiny.

Creole Chocolate Cheese Cake

1 ½ cups crushed
   chocolate cookies
¼ teaspoon nutmeg

½ cup melted butter
Filling
Grated chocolate

Mix together crushed cookies, nutmeg, and butter. Firmly press on bottom of 9-inch springform pan. Pour Filling over crust. Bake at 300° for 60 minutes. Turn off oven; leave in oven 30 minutes with door closed. Open oven door, and leave cake in until cool. Sprinkle with grated chocolate.

Filling:
6 ounces dark
   chocolate
2 (8-ounce) packages
   cream cheese
¾ cup sugar

3 eggs
1 ¼ tablespoons cocoa
1 ½ tablespoons vanilla
1 cup sour cream

Melt chocolate in small bowl over water. Press cream cheese through a strainer, and beat in sugar until smooth. Add eggs one at a time, beating well after each. Combine melted chocolate, cocoa, vanilla, and sour cream. Beat cream cheese mixture, and fold into chocolate mixture. Pour into crust.

Yield: 8 servings
Britt Shockley

Chocolate Praline Pie

3 eggs
1 cup light corn syrup
½ cup sugar
⅓ cup margarine
2 tablespoons praline
   liqueur or amaretto

1 cup pecan halves
¾ cup semi-sweet
   chocolate chips,
   divided
1 uncooked 9-inch pie
   shell

In a medium mixing bowl, slightly beat eggs with a hand beater. Add corn syrup, sugar, margarine, and praline liqueur. Stir constantly until sugar is dissolved. Add pecan halves and ½ cup chocolate chips. Spoon into pie shell. Cover edges with aluminum foil to prevent burning. Bake at 350° for 25 minutes. Remove foil; sprinkle remaining chocolate chips on top of pie. Bake an additional 20 to 25 minutes or until knife inserted near center comes out clean. Do not over bake. Cool thoroughly on a wire rack before serving.

Yield: 8 servings
Donald R. Hebert

Fig Tree Cake

1 cup boiling water
2 teaspoons baking
  soda
1½ cups sugar
1 scant cup salad oil
1 cup canned figs,
  mashed
2 large eggs, beaten
½ teaspoon ground
  cloves

½ teaspoon cinnamon
1 teaspoon ginger
2½ cups all-purpose
  flour
Pinch of salt
½ cup roasted pecans,
  chopped
Zest of 1 orange

This was one of Roy's mother's favorite desserts. The recipe makes a good cane syrup cake if you substitute cane syrup for figs.

In a small bowl, mix boiling water and soda; set aside. In a large bowl, cream sugar, salad oil, and figs. Add water/soda, beaten eggs, spices, flour, salt, pecans, and orange zest. Mix well. Pour into greased Bundt or 9x9x2-inch pan. Bake at 350° for 40 minutes or until wooden pick tests clean.

Yield: 4 to 6 servings
Roy Lyons

Dust with powdered sugar or serve with vanilla ice cream.

Pralines

1 pound unsalted
  margarine
1 quart heavy cream
4 cups sugar

2 (16-ounce) boxes
  light brown sugar
9 cups pecan pieces
4 tablespoons vanilla
  extract

Place all ingredients (except vanilla) in heavy saucepan, and cook on high until mixture reaches 234°. Stir constantly. Remove from heat, and add vanilla. Stir vigorously until mixture becomes thick and starts to lose its sheen. Drop by spoonfuls on wax paper.

Yield: 36 servings
William Menard

For easier handling, use ice-cream scoop to portion. Place newspaper under wax paper.

secretsecretsecretsecretsecretsecretsecretsecretsecretsecretsecretsecret

At the first signs of autumn turn freshly shelled pecans into a delicious melt-in-your-mouth sensation. Peanuts work well in this recipe also. And for a different twist, add 3 cups toasted coconut to the pecan recipe.

Louisiana Pecan Pie

³/₄ **cup vegetable**
shortening
1 ¹/₃ **cups all-purpose**
flour
¹/₂ **teaspoon light corn**
syrup

³/₄ **teaspoon salt**
¹/₄ **cup ice water**
1 ¹/₂ **cups pecans**
Filling

In a large bowl, cut shortening into flour until the mixture resembles small peas. In a small bowl combine corn syrup, salt, and ice water. Add to flour mixture. Beat with an electric mixer on medium speed until well blended, 2 to 3 minutes. Cover the dough with plastic wrap, and refrigerate until firm, about 1 hour. On a lightly floured surface, roll dough ¹/₄ inch thick. Line a 9-inch glass pie plate with dough, and spread pecans on surface of pie dough. Pour Filling into prepared pie shell, and bake at 325° for 75 minutes or until golden brown.

Filling:
4 **eggs**
1 **cup sugar**
3 **tablespoons melted**
unsalted butter

1 **tablespoon vanilla**
extract
1 **cup light corn syrup**

In a bowl, beat eggs for 1 minute. Add sugar, butter, vanilla, and corn syrup. Beat until smooth.

Yield: 6 to 8 servings
Patrick Mould C.E.C.

SILVER—1987

Bill developed this for his wife, Marie, who is a chocoholic.

Hot Fudge Pie

¹/₂ **cup graham cracker**
crumbs
¹/₂ **cup pecans**
1 **egg, beaten**
¹/₂ **cup flour**
¹/₂ **cup sugar**

4 **tablespoons butter or**
margarine
12 **ounces milk**
chocolate chips
2 **tablespoons praline**
liqueur

Spray pie pan with nonstick spray. Sprinkle graham cracker crumbs over bottom, then pecans over cracker crumbs. In bowl, combine beaten egg, flour, and sugar. Mix well. In heavy saucepan, melt butter. Add chocolate chips. Heat until melted, stirring constantly. Remove from heat, and stir in liqueur. Add chocolate mixture to dry ingredients. Mix well, and pour into pie pan. Bake at 350° about 30 minutes and cool.

Yield: 10 servings
William M. O'Dea C.E.C., A.A.C.

Red Velvet Cake

½ cup shortening
1½ cups sugar
2 eggs
1 teaspoon salt
1 teaspoon vanilla
  extract
1¼ teaspoons butter
  flavor extract
3 tablespoons cocoa
  powder

3 tablespoons red food
  coloring
2½ cups sifted cake
  flour
1 cup buttermilk
1 teaspoon baking soda
1 teaspoon vinegar
Frosting

The original version of this recipe called for lard, barn eggs, and milk with cream intact.

Cream shortening, sugar, eggs, salt, and extracts. Make a paste of cocoa and food coloring. Add to first mixture. Alternately add flour and buttermilk. Mix baking soda and vinegar in a small bowl. Add to batter and blend. Pour batter into 3 (9-inch) greased and floured cake pans. Bake at 350° for 25 to 35 minutes. Cool on wire rack before frosting.

Frosting:
1 cup milk
3 tablespoons flour
½ teaspoon salt
1 cup shortening

1 cup sugar
2 teaspoons vanilla
  extract

Cook milk, flour, and salt until thick, stirring constantly. Cool mixture. Cream shortening and sugar. Add vanilla, mix well. Add milk and flour mixture to mixer, and beat until light and fluffy.

Yield: 16 servings
Lonnie B. Pope, Sr.

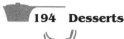

BRONZE—1986

Pecan Cake

2½ pounds yellow cake mix
3 eggs
1 cup Sprite or 7-Up
1 cup water

½ cup finely ground pecans
Filling
Frosting

Combine all ingredients in a medium bowl, and mix well. Pour batter into 2 (9-inch) cake pans. Bake at 350° for 30 minutes or until cake tests done. Remove from heat; set aside, and let cool. To assemble, cut each cake in half lengthwise. Spoon some of the syrup Filling over first layer cake; then add pecan mixture. Add next layer cake, and continue process with remaining layers. After all filling mixture has been used, spread the entire cake with Frosting.

Filling:

1 cup water
1 cup sugar
2 tablespoons butter
1 tablespoon vanilla

2 cups ground pecans
1 (14-ounce) can condensed milk

Combine first 4 ingredients in a small saucepan. Bring to boil over high heat. Reduce heat to medium. Cook 5 minutes, stirring often. Remove from heat, and set aside. In a small bowl, mix ground pecans and condensed milk. Set aside.

Frosting:

2 (3-ounce) packages cream cheese
4 ounces margarine

3 cups confectioners' sugar
1 cup ground pecans

Combine ingredients in a small bowl, and mix well.

Yield: 10 servings
Enola Prudhomme

Louisiana Berry Royale

BRONZE—1984

8 tablespoons flour
1 egg
1 egg yolk
2 tablespoons melted
  butter
¼ teaspoon salt

16 tablespoons milk
Crêpe Filling
Custard
1¼ cups whipping
  cream, whipped

Replace
heavy cream with
half-and-half, but
you will sacrifice
some flavor.

Combine flour, egg, egg yolk, butter, salt, and milk. Mix until smooth. Strain. Let set for 30 minutes before making crêpes. After crêpes are done, set aside. Fill crêpes with soaked-berry Filling. Fold crêpes into triangles. Assemble the royal in layers alternating filled crêpes and Custard in a springform pan. Chill. Unmold when firm, and cut into wedges. Top with whipped cream and more of the liqueur.

Crêpe Filling:
2 cups assorted
  Louisiana berries
  (strawberries,
  raspberries or
  blackberries)

Fruit-flavored liqueur

Soak berries overnight in liqueur. Fill crêpes with soaked berries. Puree any remaining berries to yield ½ cup for use in custard.

Custard:
2 envelopes unflavored
  gelatin
½ cup Chardonnay,
  divided
¼ cup flavored liqueur

1 tablespoon fresh
  lemon juice
½ cup sugar
¼ teaspoon salt
½ cup berry puree

For custard, dissolve gelatin into ⅓ cup of Chardonnay over low heat. Do not boil. Transfer to a small bowl. Heat remaining wine, liqueur, lemon juice, and sugar until dissolved. Add salt. Stir into gelatin mixture. Cool in an ice bath until it starts to set. Fold in berry puree to give a marbling effect.

Yield: 12 servings
Bryan Richard

Having fresh berries and macerating them overnight makes quite a difference in this recipe.

SILVER—1990

Chocolate Meringue Torte

5 egg whites	2 ounces cocoa powder
¹/₂ cup sugar	Chocolate Mousse
1 cup confectioners sugar	Chocolate Garnish

Whip egg whites until soft. Fold in sugar, and whip until firm. Sift confectioners' sugar and cocoa powder, and fold in. Fill a pastry bag with a #4 round tip with meringue. Pipe meringue in 2 (9-inch) circles on a cookie sheet lined with parchment paper. Bake at 200° for 120 minutes or until meringue is completely dry. To assemble cake, place 1 layer of meringue on a cardboard circle. Using a spatula, spread a layer of Chocolate Mousse onto the meringue. Place the next meringue layer on top and cover the top and sides with the remaining mousse. Refrigerate for 1 hour. Decorate cake with Chocolate Garnish. Begin by wrapping the side of the cake. For the top of the cake, try to get the ribbon into a fan shape by placing your thumb against one edge of the chocolate ribbon's edge. Form a circle with the least pleated strips of chocolate. Place in center of cake and form more ribbons around the center fan.

Chocolate Mousse:

¹/₂ pound semi-sweet chocolate	3 eggs, separated
1 ¹/₂ ounces butter	¹/₂ cup sugar
	¹/₂ quart heavy cream

Melt semi-sweet chocolate and butter. Fold in egg yolks. Whip egg whites until soft; then whip in sugar until firm. Fold into chocolate mixture. Whip heavy cream until stiff; fold into chocolate mixture.

Chocolate Garnish:
¹/₂ pound semi-sweet chocolate

Melt chocolate in a double boiler. Spread a very thin layer of chocolate onto the back side of a cookie sheet. Refrigerate until set but not hard. Using a putty knife nearly horizontal to the baking pan, scrape off a band of chocolate. The chocolate should form a ribbon.

Yield: 10 servings
Sue Anne Zamani C.E.P.C.

Lagniappe

First You Make a Roux

8 cups oil
9 cups flour
½ cup diced onion

¼ cup diced green pepper
2 tablespoons minced fresh garlic

Use either a magnalite pot or black pot. Be sure the pot is clean. Anything left in the pot will burn, and mess up the roux. Heat the oil first. Heat it until the point where it just begins to smoke. Quickly, but carefully, add small amounts of flour. (Add flour, stir, etc. until all is added). Be absolutely sure to stir continuously from the second you put flour into the oil until the desired color is reached. Make sure that it does not stick. Stir and scrape the bottom of the pot at all times. When you have reached the color needed, remove the pot from the fire, and continue to stir. Add the vegetables, and continue to stir until the vegetables no longer sizzle and the roux has cooled down. Allow the roux to settle for about 30 to 45 minutes. The excess oil will rise to the top. Skim off the oil before adding to whatever dish you are preparing. Always measure the roux exactly.

Yield: 7 cups
Roy Lyons

Always try to cook the roux as consistent as humanly possible. The character of each dish changes with the inconsistency of each roux. For gumbo, the color should be dark brown only. For crawfish bisque, the color should be peanut colored. For stews, the color should be between peanut and dark brown.

A Good All-Purpose Seasoning

¾ cup granulated garlic
¾ cup salt
6 tablespoons dry mustard
6 tablespoons red pepper
6 tablespoons black pepper
2 tablespoons white pepper
1 tablespoon allspice

6 tablespoons Hungarian paprika
2 tablespoons celery seed
¼ cup coriander
1 tablespoon cumin
6 tablespoons sumac (optional)
2 tablespoons oregano

Mix all ingredients together. Use for boiling seafood or just shake on foods to give them that Cajun flavor.

Yield: about 4 cups
Kenneth Koval

Crawfish: A Guide

When spring approaches, most Louisianans turn to that unique seafood delight — crawfish. These small, tasty shellfish have been a tradition with folks in South Louisiana for more than two centuries. Although freshwater crawfish are found in every state, Louisiana grows and processes about 90% of all crawfish harvested in the United States, and consumes about 80% of that.

Most commercial producers harvest crawfish in special wire traps baited with fish, such as shad. Traps are run daily if the weather permits. Crawfish are sacked in mesh onion sacks for delivery to processors, restaurants, or retail markets.

Crawfishing is also a popular family sport in the state. With abundant shallow waters near roads and highways, crawfishing areas are easily accessible. Recreational crawfishermen often use small lift nets make from a square panel of cotton netting and wire bows. Bait, such as chicken necks, is secured in the middle of the net. Because the crawfish are not restrained by the net — except at the moment of capture — nets must be checked every 10 to 15 minutes. After a good day of crawfishing, a crawfish boil will soon be taking place.

Availability

Live crawfish and fresh tail meat are usually available from December until June. However, March, April, and May are the months when crawfish are most plentiful and are of the best quality. Although fresh crawfish and crawfish meat are seasonal, frozen crawfish tail meat and frozen whole crawfish can usually be obtained throughout the year.

Processing

Whether you catch your own or purchase a sack of crawfish, it is important that they remain alive until time for cooking. Crawfish decompose rapidly after death. Although not necessarily a health hazard, if cooked properly, decomposed dead crawfish have mushy, discolored meat unsuitable for consumption.

When tightly packed in onion sacks and kept cool and moist with plenty of air, crawfish can be kept alive out of water for a considerable period of time. Never place live crawfish in small airtight containers, in small containers full of water, or in direct sunlight. Such conditions will quickly kill them. In addition, never place heavy objects on the sack of crawfish or handle the sack roughly. This could crush and injure many of them.

Wash and inspect your crawfish carefully. Discard debris, such as bait and dead crawfish, and remove mud and dirt by washing. Many people add salt to the wash water in order to "purge" the crawfish. This practice is unnecessary and, in fact, just puts the crawfish under stress.

Cooking

Boiling is the most popular method of cooking crawfish for home consumption. One way of boiling crawfish is as follows:

• Bring pot of water to a rolling boil. (A good rule of thumb: Use 1 gallon of water for every 2 pounds of crawfish.)

- Carefully pour the live crawfish into the boiling water. The crawfish are killed quickly upon contact. Make sure all crawfish are submerged in the water for uniform cooking.

- When the water comes to a boil again, begin the timing. Cooking times depend upon how the crawfish will be eaten.

    a) If using crawfish in other dishes where you will need to peel them, remove crawfish when water resumes boiling. No seasoning is necessary.

    b) For the traditional crawfish boil where they are peeled and eaten immediately, boil the crawfish for 10 minutes after the second boil starts; then turn off the heat, and soak the crawfish 10 to 15 minutes longer. Season the water well with onions, lemon wedges, red pepper, garlic, commercial crab boil, and salt before cooking. Cool crawfish slightly before peeling; refrigerate those that will not be eaten immediately.

Eating

1. Upon cooking, crawfish become bright red.

2. Separate the tail from the head by slightly twisting and firmly pulling the tail from the head. Discard the head.

3. Hold the tail between the forefinger and thumb, and squeeze. You should hear the shell crack.

4. Grasp the first three shell segments from the side, and loosen by lifting up and pulling around the meat. Discard this part.

5. Firmly grasp the last segment and tail fin between the thumb and forefinger of one hand and the meat with the other hand, and gently pull. The meat should slide out of the shell, and the vein should pull free from the meat. Crawfish meat is now ready for eating, freezing, or adding to your favorite dish.

•　•　•　•　•

Information from Dwight Landreneau, Aquaculture Agent, Louisiana State University Agricultural Center; Louisiana Cooperative Extension Service.

Cajun Glossary

Andouille sausage: a spicy, heavily smoked sausage made from pork chitterlings and tripe

Basil chiffonade: three or four basil leaves stacked upon one another, rolled tightly, and then cut into 1/4-inch strips

Bisque: a thick rich soup usually consisting of pureed seafood and cream

Cèpes: pale brown delicious edible mushrooms found in woodland areas; difficult to find in U.S. markets

Chow Chow: onion and hot pepper relish

Cracklin: delicious crunchy pieces of either pork or poultry fat after it has been rendered

Crawfish: freshwater crustaceans, mostly harvested in Louisiana, that are similar in appearance to lobsters but only 3 to 6 inches long

Étouffée (smothered): a spicy Cajun stew of vegetables and seafood, especially crawfish

Filé: powdered sassafras leaves used to thicken and season soups, stews, and gumbos

Fleuron: small half-moon-shaped, baked puff pastry garnish

Fond du Veal: veal stock, gently reduced

Gumbo: a soup thickened with roux or okra, or both

Jambalaya: a Creole dish consisting of rice that has been cooked with seafood or meat and seasoned with spices and herbs

Javelina: wild boar

Mirepoix: a mixture of diced carrots, celery, onions and herbs sautéed in butter. It's used to season sauces, soups, and stews

Oyster Liquor: the natural juices present in the oyster shell. Clam juice can be substituted

Roulades: a turban shape made from a fish fillet

Roux: a mixture of flour and fat that's slowly cooked over low heat; it's used to thicken soups and stews

Sachet Bag of Herbs: parsley, sage, rosemary, and thyme

Seafood Stock: traditional stock made from a combination of shrimp shells, crawfish shells, and fish heads and bones

Tasso: firm, smoky, flavorful cured pork that is used for seasoning·

Culinary Classic Judges Share Their Recipes

PAUL PRUDHOMME: A best-selling author and successful restaurateur in New Orleans, Prudhomme introduced Louisiana cooking to America. He helped instill the idea — and generate support — for the very first Culinary Classic held in Lafayette.

This wonderful dish has just a hint of the exotic (because of the fresh ginger and tamari sauce), and may make you think of faraway places. But it couldn't be easier to prepare, so you can enjoy it at home any time.

Hot and Sweet Turkey

Seasoning Mix (mix first 4 ingredients):
1 tablespoon plus 1 teaspoon Chef Paul Prudhomme's Poultry Magic®
½ teaspoon ground ginger
¼ teaspoon ground nutmeg
¼ teaspoon ground coriander
1 pound turkey breast, cut into 2x¼-inch julienne strips
3 tablespoons cornstarch
2½ cups defatted chicken stock, in all
¼ cup thinly sliced fresh ginger
1 small onion, peeled and cut into julienne strips
¾ cup carrots, scrubbed and sliced diagonally ¼ inch thick
¾ cup julienne red bell peppers
¾ cup julienne yellow bell peppers
¾ cup julienne green bell peppers
2 teaspoons thinly sliced fresh garlic
¼ cup tamari (see note)
¼ cup balsamic vinegar
1 (8-ounce) can tomato sauce
6 (1-gram) packets artificial sweetener, optional
4 cups cooked long-gram white rice
3 tablespoons Chef Paul Prudhomme's Magic Pepper Sauce

Combine the seasoning mix ingredients in a small bowl. Sprinkle all surfaces of the turkey evenly with 2 teaspoons of the seasoning mix and rub it in well. Dissolve the cornstarch in 4 tablespoons of the stock and set aside. Preheat a heavy 12-inch skillet, preferably nonstick, over high heat to 350°, about 5 minutes. Add the turkey, stir, and cook until it starts to brown, about 2 minutes. Add the fresh ginger and onions, stir and cook for 2 minutes. Add the remaining vegetables and seasoning mix, and cook for 3 minutes. Stir in the tamari and vinegar, and cook 2 minutes. Stir in the tomato sauce and remaining stock, bring to a boil, and cook 2 minutes. Add the cornstarch mixture, cook for 2 minutes, remove from the heat, and, if desired, add artificial sweetener. Serve over the rice and add pepper sauce.

Tamari is a very flavorful kind of soy sauce, available in specialty markets and the international or ethnic food sections of many supermarkets. If you cannot find it where you shop, substitute the best soy sauce available.

© Copyright 1993 by Paul Prudhomme
From **Fork in the Road**

JOHN FOLSE: Respected around the world as an authority on Cajun and Creole cuisine and culture, Folse owns Lafitte's Landing in Donaldsonville, Louisiana, and has been associated with the Classic for many years as a competitor and committee participant. Folse is 1994 national president of the American Culinary Federation.

Though there are hundreds of variations of the Southern Pecan Pie, Folse has tried diligently to come up with his own rendition that is lighter and less sweet. The addition of orange juice in the place of brown sugar makes this recipe more appealing.

Orange Cane Syrup Pecan Pie

5 whole eggs
½ cup sugar
1 cup light Karo syrup
1 tablespoon sugar cane syrup
¼ cup fresh squeezed orange
  juice

1 tablespoon grated orange peel
1 tablespoon flour
¾ cup chopped pecans
1 (9-inch) unbaked pie shell
16 pecan halves

Preheat oven to 350°. In a large mixing bowl, combine eggs and sugar, whipping well with a wire whisk. Do not overbeat. Add Karo and cane syrups, and blend into the egg mixture. Pour in orange juice and orange peel, and sprinkle in flour. Blend until all is well incorporated. Add chopped pecans, fold once or twice into the mixture, and pour into pie shell. Place the pecan halves in a circular pattern on the outer edge of the pie. Place on a cookie sheet, and cover with parchment paper. Bake approximately 1 hour, and check for doneness. It is best to cool the pie overnight. Slice into 8 equal portions.

Yield: 8 servings

FRANK BRIGTSEN: As chef/owner of Brigtsen's Restaurant in New Orleans, Brigtsen has been a judge for the Classic for many years. Here he shares a soup recipe that has been his restaurant's most popular one over the years.

Butternut Shrimp Bisque

5 tablespoons unsalted butter, divided
2 cups chopped yellow onions
1 bay leaf
4 cups butternut squash, peeled, deseeded, and diced into 1/2-inch cubes
2 cups peeled fresh shrimp
2 1/4 teaspoons salt
1/8 teaspoon ground white pepper

3/8 teaspoon ground cayenne pepper
1/4 teaspoon whole leaf dried sweet basil
1/4 teaspoon whole leaf dried thyme
1/4 teaspoon minced fresh garlic
1/2 cup shrimp stock
6 cups heavy whipping cream
1/2 teaspoon fresh sweet basil, very finely chopped

Heat a 4-quart cast aluminum saucepan over medium-high heat. Add 3 tablespoons of unsalted butter, onions, and bay leaf. Cook onions, stirring constantly, until they just begin to brown, about 3 to 4 minutes. Reduce heat to medium, and add butternut squash. Cook this mixture, stirring occasionally, until squash begins to soften and turn brown, about 7 to 8 minutes. Reduce heat to low, and add 1 tablespoon of unsalted butter and peeled shrimp. Cook this mixture, stirring occasionally, until the shrimp turn pink, about 2 to 3 minutes. Add salt, white pepper, cayenne pepper, dried basil, dried thyme, and garlic. Cook this mixture for 3 to 4 minutes, stirring constantly and scraping the bottom and sides of the saucepan with a metal spoon. This procedure will intensify the taste of the final product. Add shrimp stock, and simmer for 2-3 minutes. Transfer this mixture to a food processor and puree. Return mixture to saucepan, and add cream. Bring to a boil; then lower heat, and simmer for 2 to 3 minutes. Just before serving, add fresh sweet basil and remaining 1 tablespoon of unsalted butter.

6 (10-ounce) portions

To make fresh shrimp stock, place shrimp heads and shells in a pot and cover with cold water. Bring to a boil, simmer for 15 minutes, and strain.

JOHNNY RIVERS: Executive chef of Walt Disney Marketplace/Pleasure Island complex, Rivers has been judging the Classic for a few years. Here he shares a recipe from *Down Home Healthy*, a cookbook he co-authored.

Black Skillet Beef With Greens & Red Potatoes

1 pound beef top round
1 ½ tablespoons Hot 'N Spicy
  Seasoning
Nonstick spray coating
8 red-skinned potatoes, halved
3 cups finely chopped onion
2 cups beef broth

2 large cloves garlic, minced
2 large carrots, peeled and cut
  into very thin strips
2 (8-ounce) bunches mustard
  greens, kale, or turnip greens,
  stems removed and coarsely
  torn

Partially freeze beef. Thinly slice across the grain into long strips ⅛ inch thick. Thoroughly coat strips with Hot 'N Spicy Seasoning. Spray a large heavy skillet (cast iron is good) with nonstick spray coating. Preheat pan over high heat. Add meat; cook, stirring, for 5 minutes. Add potatoes, onion, broth, and garlic. Cook, covered, over medium heat for 20 minutes. Stir in carrots, lay greens over top, and cook, covered, until carrots are tender, about 15 minutes. Serve in large serving bowl, with crusty bread for dunking.

6 servings

LARRY FORGIONE: Celebrity chef for the Classic and winner of the 1991 Paul Prudhomme medal, Forgione is chef/owner of An American Place Restaurant in New York City and the Beekman Arms in Rhinebeck, New York. He prepared this recipe for a demonstration during the Classic.

Cedar Planked Salmon

2 untreated pieces cedar shingles
  or shims
1 teaspoon salt
¼ teaspoon freshly ground black
  pepper

¼ teaspoon dry mustard
1 tablespoon unsalted butter,
  room temperature
4 (6-ounce) salmon fillets,
  skinned and boned

Mix together the salt, pepper and mustard, Brush the top of the fillets with a little butter and then sprinkle both sides with dry mustard mixture. Preheat the broiler. Soak the shingles in cold water for 5 to 10 minutes and then put them under the hot broiler — 4 to 5 inches from the heat sauce — for 2 to 3 minutes until browned on one side. Carefully take the shingles from the broiler. Immediately, so that the shingles do not cool, lay 2 fillets on the browned side of each shingle. Return the shingles to the broiler, and cook the fish for about 5 minutes. Take the shingles from the broiler, and lift the salmon from them. To serve, place 3 to 4 tablespoons of Soft Pumpkin Corn Pudding onto plate, top with salmon, spoon Pumpkin Seed Vinaigrette around the salmon, and sprinkle with toasted pumpkin seeds.

Soft Pumpkin Corn Pudding:

2 tablespoons lightly salted
  butter
1 tablespoon minced garlic
1 cup fresh or frozen corn kernels
1 teaspoon ground cumin
½ teaspoon ground allspice
Pinch of cayenne

2 cups milk
1 cup fresh pumpkin puree
⅝ cup stone-ground cornmeal
Salt and freshly ground black
  pepper to taste
2 tablespoons finely sliced fresh
  chives or scallions

Melt the butter in a 2-quart saucepan over medium heat until it begins to foam and turn light brown. Add the garlic and corn kernels. Cook for 2 to 3 minutes, and season with the cumin, allspice, and cayenne. Continue to cook another minute, and add the milk and pumpkin puree. Bring the mixture to a simmer. Stirring continuously, slowly add the cornmeal to the pan. As the pudding thickens, lower the heat and continue to cook, stirring, for 5 to 6 minutes longer. The pudding will be the consistency of thick oatmeal or cream of wheat. Season with salt and pepper. Add the chives, and set aside.

Pumpkin Seed Vinaigrette:

½ cup shelled pumpkin seeds
¼ teaspoon minced garlic
½ teaspoon turmeric
½ cup plus 2 tablespoons apple
  cider vinegar, divided

¾ cup seed or nut oil
Salt and freshly ground black
  pepper to taste

(Continued on next page)

Cedar Planked Salmon (continued)

Preheat oven to 325°. Spread the pumpkin seeds in a shallow pan, and lightly toast them for 3 to 4 minutes in the oven. Put the toasted seeds, garlic, turmeric, and ½ cup vinegar in a small saucepan. (Reserve 2 tablespoons of the seeds for garnish.) Cook over medium heat for 2 to 3 minutes. Remove the pan from the heat and whisk in the oil. Stir in the remaining 2 tablespoons vinegar, and season with salt and pepper. Puree the mixture in a blender or food processor for only 1 minute, set aside, and keep warm.

Yield: 4 servings

BEANY MACGREGOR: Executive chef for Planet Hollywood, Inc., and a Louisiana native, MacGregor shares his White Chocolate Bread Pudding with Whiskey Sauce.

White Chocolate Bread Pudding

³/₄ **pounds stale French bread**
³/₄ **pound white chocolate**
¹/₂ **cup milk**
¹/₄ **pound granulated sugar**
1 ¹/₄ **cups heavy cream**

2 teaspoons vanilla extract
3 egg yolks
Nonstick cooking spray
Butter
Whiskey Sauce

Cut French bread and white chocolate into ³/₄-inch cubes. Heat milk, sugar, heavy cream, and vanilla. When warm, stir in egg yolks. Add white chocolate chunks, and stir until melted. Add mixture to bread, and mix well. Let soak for 30 minutes. Spray 8-ounce cups with nonstick cooking spray. Place 8 ounces of mixture into each cup, and cook in water bath at 350°, covered, for 45 minutes. Remove cover, brush with butter and cook 15 minutes more. To serve: Unmold from cups. Pour 3 ounces of Whiskey Sauce on top of bread pudding. Sprinkle with white chocolate curls.

Whiskey Sauce:
9 ounces butter
2 ¹/₄ **cups sugar**

¹/₄ **bottle (750 ml) bourbon**
2 eggs

Cream butter and sugar together in stockpot over low heat until smooth. Carefully add bourbon to sugar mixture while stirring. Cook 3 minutes over medium heat. Whisk eggs with 4 ounces bourbon mixture; then gradually add this mixture back into the rest of the bourbon mixture. Strain through a fine mesh. Serve over bread pudding.

Yield: 5 individual servings

BRIAN FOLEY: Executive chef of Disney's Port Orleans and Dixie Landings, Walt Disney World Resorts and a judge of the Classic, Foley shares a favorite recipe from Walt Disney World.

Scallops Mardi Gras

20 ounces sea scallops, cleaned
1 ounce Cajun spice
1 ounce butter, clarified
20 ounces tri-colored linguine,
  cooked al dente

1 pint Tomato Basil Cream
2 ounces diced red peppers
1 teaspoon chopped parsley
2 tablespoons Parmesan cheese

Clean scallops by removing the muscle; toss scallops in the Cajun seasoning. Heat butter in a large skillet, and sauté the scallops until cooked through. Do not overcook. Cook the tri-colored linguine until al dente; drain and place approximately 5 ounces on a warm plate. Pour the Tomato Basil Cream over the pasta. Top with approximately 5 ounces of scallops; then sprinkle with the diced red peppers, chopped parsley, and Parmesan cheese.

Yield: 4 servings

Tomato Basil Cream:
2 cups half-and-half
1 cup heavy cream
¾ cup tomato puree
2 tablespoons basil, chopped

Garlic powder to taste
Salt to taste
White pepper to taste
1 cup roux

Combine the half-and-half, heavy cream, tomato puree, basil, and garlic powder. Bring to a boil, gradually whisk in the roux. Cook five minutes until smooth; season with salt and white pepper to taste. Strain the sauce, keep warm.

Yield: 1 quart

Prepare the roux by melting 4 ounces of butter in a heavy skillet; add 4 ounces of flour. Stir until the butter is absorbed; heat on low for 5 minutes. Do not brown. Cool.

Reprinted with the permission of
The Walt Disney Company

KEITH KEOGH: Research and Development Executive Chef for EPCOT '94, Walt Disney World Company, Keogh has twice been named Florida's Seafood Chef of the Year. He served as president of the American Culinary Federation from 1991 to 1993. Keogh is one of ACF's approved judges for the Classic, and 1992 and 1996 Culinary Olympic Team Manager.

Quesadillas Stuffed With Chorizo Sausage

12 ounces chorizo sausage
1 tablespoon oil or lard
1/4 cup finely diced white onion
1/2 cup potatoes, cooked and
   finely diced
1 medium tomato (peeled,
   seeded, and finely diced)

2 jalapeño peppers (optional)
Freshly ground black pepper
Salt to taste
8 (6-inch) flour tortillas
2 eggs, beaten lightly (egg wash)
3 cups oil
Avocado-Sour Cream Dip

Remove skin from the sausage; chop fine. In preheated sauté pan, add 1 tablespoon oil; when hot, add sausage meat and brown. Discard almost all the fat. Add onion, and sauté for approximately 2 minutes. Then add potato and tomato (and pepper, if desired). Sauté for about 2 more minutes, and season well. Take off the burner, and set aside. Let cool. Cut tortilla shells in half, and put about 1 ounce (about 1 teaspoon) in each half. Brush exposed shell with the egg wash, and press until bonded well. Heat 3 cups oil in a 2-inch skillet to about 300°, and deep fry quesadillas until golden brown on both sides, approximately 2 to 3 minutes. Remove from oil, and drain on paper towels. Serve with Avocado-Sour Cream Dip.

Avocado-Sour Cream Dip:
1 ripe avocado, peeled and
   mashed
1 medium tomato, peeled and
   diced
1/2 cup sour cream
1/2 small white onion, finely
   chopped
1 jalapeño pepper, seeded and
   finely chopped
Salt and pepper to taste

Tabasco sauce to taste
Worcestershire sauce to taste
2 sprigs of coriander, finely
   chopped
Pinch of sugar
1/2 lemon, squeezed

Mix all ingredients well, and pile high in serving dish. Place avocado pit in center to prevent dip from turning dark.

Yield: 4 servings

TONY DONNELLY: Executive chef and Food and Beverage Director of Polynesian Walt Disney World Resorts, Donnelly served as judge and seminar participant for the 1993 Classic.

Plantation Bean Soup

½ cup diced Spanish onion
½ cup diced celery
¼ pound andouille sausage, sliced
1 ounce tasso, diced
2 tablespoons butter
1 pound Barzl 16-bean soup mix

1½ ounces ham bouillon
1 (1-pound) ham bone (optional)
3 quarts water
1 tablespoon Tabasco sauce
1 tablespoon ground white pepper

In stockpot, sauté onion, celery, andouille, and tasso in butter, until onion is transparent. Add bean mix, ham bouillon, and ham bone; mix well. Stir in water, Tabasco, and white pepper. Simmer for 2 hours, stirring occasionally. Adjust seasoning. Serve with French bread.

JOE CAHN: Of New Orleans School of Cooking, Cahn has been involved with the Classic as presenter and master of ceremonies. He shares the treasures of the region directly to visitor's homes through their kitchens.

Heart Healthy Jambalaya

1 chicken, cut up or boned, skinless
¼ cup olive oil
1½ pounds turkey sausage
4 cups chopped onion
2 cups chopped celery
2 cups chopped green pepper
1 tablespoon chopped garlic

5 cups stock or flavored water
Joe's Stuff seasoning or any all-purpose seasoning
2 cups chopped green onions
Kitchen Bouquet for color
4 cups long grain rice
Green onions and chopped tomatoes (optional)

Season and brown chicken in olive oil over medium high heat. Add sausage to pot, and sauté with chicken. Remove both from pot. Sauté onion, celery, green pepper, and garlic to the tenderness that you desire. Return chicken and sausage to pot. Add stock, Joe's Stuff and other desired seasonings; bring to boil. If using Kitchen Bouquet for browning, add 1 to 2 tablespoons. (For red Jambalaya, add approximately ¼ cup paprika, and you may want to use ½ stock and ⅓ tomato juice or V-8 for your liquid.) Add rice, and return to boil. Cover and reduce heat to simmer. Cook for a total of 30 minutes. After 10 minutes of cooking, remove cover, and quickly turn rice from top to bottom completely. Add green onions and chopped tomatoes if desired. (For seafood Jambalaya, follow the first two steps and then add seafood.)

16 (1-cup) servings

Restaurants and Food Service Providers

Sponsoring chefs from Acadiana for the Culinary Classic

BARACCA'S ITALIAN GRILL

BROUSSARD'S CATERING

CAFE ACADIE (Crowley)

CAFE VERMILIONVILLE

CHARLIE G'S SEAFOOD GRILL & BAR

CHRIS' PO-BOYS

CITY CLUB OF LAFAYETTE

EVANGELINE STEAK HOUSE AND SEAFOOD RESTAURANT

HUB CITY DINER

i MONELLI RESTAURANT

LAFAYETTE GENERAL MEDICAL CENTER, Dietary Department

LAFAYETTE REGIONAL TECHNICAL INSTITUTE, Department of Culinary Arts

LAFAYETTE HILTON AND TOWERS

OAKBOURNE COUNTRY CLUB

PETROLEUM CLUB OF LAFAYETTE

PREJEAN'S RESTAURANT

PRUDHOMME'S CAJUN CAFE

RANDOL'S SEAFOOD RESTAURANT

REHABILITATION HOSPITAL OF LAFAYETTE, Dietary Department

RIVERSIDE INN

RUTH'S CHRIS STEAK HOUSE

THE DESSERT COMPANY

THE GORDON

THE HOTEL ACADIANA

THE LANDING

THE OYSTER REEF SEAFOOD RESTAURANT

USL HOSPITALITY / MANAGEMENT PROGRAM

Appreciation to Sponsors of the Culinary Classic

Acadiana Bottling

Awards and Trophies of Lafayette

Bano Quality Produce

Borden, Inc.

Bruce Foods Corp.

Cardiovascular Institute of the South

Cintas Services

Community Coffee

Conco Food Services

Courtesy Motors

Doerle Food Services

Edward Don & Co., Inc.

Hemophilia Foundation of Acadiana

Joe Cahn's New Orleans School of Cooking

Joe Christiana Food Distributor

John Folse & Company

Junior League of Lafayette

KACY/KSMB

KADN TV 15

KATC TV 3

Keller's Bakery

Kentwood Water

Kinko's

KLFY TV 10

KMDL

KPEL/KTDY

KXKC

Lafayette General Medical Center

Lafayette Hilton and Towers

Langlinais Bakery

Lou Ana Foods, Inc.

Louisiana Seafood Exchange

Magnolia Marketing & Reliable Marketing Companies

Marshal's of Lafayette

McIlhenny Company

Medical Center of Southwest Louisiana

Our Lady of Lourdes Regional Medical Center

Paul Prudhomme's K-Paul's Louisiana Enterprises

Poupart Bakery

Ronnie Kole Entertainment Productions

Sysco Food Services

The Hotel Acadiana

The Times of Acadiana

The Daily Advertiser

Tony Chachere's Creole Foods of Opelousas

Trans La Gas Company

Tyson

University of Southwestern Louisiana School of Human Resources

Women's & Children's Hospital

Walt Disney World, with special thanks to Duncan Dickson, Director of College Relations, Professional and International Staffing, and Chef Mickey, Orlando, FL

Suppliers of Cajun Ingredients

SEAFOOD: Alligator, Crabmeat, Crawfish (softshell), Crawfish, Redfish, Shellfish, Turtle Meat

Louisiana Premium Seafoods, Inc.
101 Railroad Avenue
P.O. Box 68
Palmetto, LA 71358
(318) 623-4232

Louisiana Seafood Exchange
920 West Pinhook Road
Lafayette, LA 70503
(318) 237-0022

CAJUN SPECIALTY MEATS: Andouille sausage, Boudin, Cracklin, Smoked Sausage, Tasso

Comeaux's Market
118 Canaan Drive
Lafayette, LA 70508
1-800-323-2492

Poche's Market
3015-A Main Highway
Breaux Bridge, LA 70517
1-800-3POCHES

John Folse & Company
2517 South Philippe Avenue
Gonzales, LA 70737
(504) 644-6000
FAX (504) 644-1295

K-Paul's Louisiana Enterprises
Magic Seasoning Blends
824 Distributors Row
P.O.Box 23342
New Orleans, LA 70183-0342
(504) 731-3690

Richard's Cajun Country
P.O. Drawer 414
Church Point, LA 70525
(318) 684-6309
FAX (318) 684-6310

Savoie's
581 Highway 742
Opelousas, LA 70570
(318) 942-7241

CAJUN SEASONINGS: Bruce Foods Seasoned Salt, Cajun Power Garlic Sauce, Louisiana Gold Pepper Sauce, Roux, Tabasco Jalapeño Sauce, Tabasco Hot Sauce, Tiger Sauce, Tony Chachere's Creole Seasoning, Try Me Tiger Sauce, Zatarain's Crab Boil Liquid Seasoning, Zatarain's Creole Seasoning

Bruce Foods Corporation
P.O. Drawer 1030
New Iberia, LA 70562
(318) 365-8101

Cajun Power Sauce Mfg., Inc.
Route 2, Box 278
Abbeville, LA 70510
(318) 893-3856

Comeaux's Market
(see address above)

John Folse & Company
(see address above)

K-Paul's Louisiana Enterprises
(see address above)

McIlhenny Co.
General Delivery
Avery Island, LA 70513
(318) 365-8173

Tony Chachere's Creole Foods
P.O. Box 1687
Opelousas, LA 70571
(318) 948-4691

Zatarain's, Inc.
P. O. Box 347
Gretna, LA 70053
(504) 367-2950

OTHER CAJUN PRODUCTS: Community Coffee, Langlinais French Bread, Lou Ana Cotton Seed Oil, Louisiana Berries, Louisiana Pecans, Louisiana Yams, Louisiana Mushrooms (Chanterelle and Shiitake), Steen's Pure Cane Syrup, Joe's Stuff

Bano Quality Produce
6930 South Choctaw Drive
Baton Rouge, LA 70806
(504) 832-0160

Bruce Foods Corporation
P.O. Drawer 1030
New Iberia, LA 70562
(318) 365-8101

Comeaux's Market
118 Canaan Drive
Lafayette, LA 70508
1-800-323-2492

Community Coffee
1760 North Bertrand Drive
Lafayette, LA 70506
(318) 234-3679

Joe Cahn's New Orleans School of Cooking
280 Hord Street
Harahan, LA 70183
1-800-237-4841

John Folse & Company
2517 South Philippe Avenue
Gonzales, LA 70737
(504) 644-6000

K-Paul's Louisiana Enterprises
Magic Seasoning Blends
824 Distributors Row
P.O.Box 23342
New Orleans, LA 70183-0342
(504) 731-3690

Keller's Bakery
1012 Jefferson Street
Lafayette, LA 70501
(318) 235-1568

Langlinais Baking Company
815 South St. Antoine Street
Lafayette, LA 70501
(318) 235-2644

Lou Ana Foods
731 North Railroad Avenue
Opelousas, LA 70570
(318) 948-6561

McIlhenny Co.
General Delivery
Avery Island, LA 70513
(318) 365-8173

Poupart Bakery
1902 West Pinhook Road
Lafayette, LA 70508
(318) 232-7921

Tony Chachere's Creole Foods
P.O. Box 1687
Opelousas, LA 70571
(318) 948-4691

C.S. Steen Syrup Mill, Inc.
P.O. Box 339
Abbeville, LA 70510
(318) 893-1654

Index

CAJUN REVELATION
American Culinary Federation, Acadiana Chapter
c/o Wimmer Cookbook Distribution
4210 B. F. Goodrich Blvd.
Memphis, TN 38118

Please send _____ copies of **Cajun Revelation**   @ $15.95 each _____
Tennessee residents add sales tax @ $1.32 each _____
Postage and handling @ $5.00 each _____
TOTAL _____

Charge to Visa (   ) or MasterCard (   ) # _____

Exp. Date _____

Signature _____

Name _____

Address _____

City _____ State _____ Zip _____

Make checks payable to **Wimmer Cookbook Distribution**
OR CALL: 1 (800) 727-1034 OR FAX: (901) 795-9806

- -

COOKBOOK LOVERS TAKE NOTE

If you've enjoyed *Cajun Revelation,* The Wimmer Companies, Inc.
has a catalog of 250 other cookbook titles that may interest you.
To recieve your free copy, write:

The Wimmer Companies, Inc.
4210 B.F. Goodrich Blvd.
Memphis, TN 38118

Or call 1-800-727-1034